Peter Tonna

WORLD'S GREATEST INFLUENCER

AUSTIN MACAULEY PUBLISHERS™

LONDON • CAMBRIDGE • NEW YORK • SHARJAH

A CIP catalogue record for this title is available from the British Library.

ISBN 9781398486386 (Paperback)
ISBN 9781398486409 (ePub e-book)

www.austinmacauley.com

First Published 2023
Austin Macauley Publishers Ltd®
1 Canada Square
Canary Wharf
London
E14 5AA

Table of Contents

Introduction

In this media tech-savvy world we live in, social media influencers have much sway in how their followers think and act. It's only a matter of time before these modern-day influencers will have had their time in the sun, and their persuasive power begins to wane because they are no longer 'cool' or relevant. Then steps up a new batch of a modern-day, appropriate and in-touch crop of influencers. As the years go on, the cycle repeats. Many years from now, the influencers of today most likely would not be given a second thought, unless they have contributed to the world in some significant and lasting way.

There is one influencer that has managed to stay relevant in every age since he came on the scene. In fact, his popularity keeps increasing even though he hasn't physically been around for over 2000 years. Quite impressive considering there was no communicative technology, social media or the World Wide Web. There was no television or viral ad campaigns. He lived a somewhat quiet life, yet his teachings and his way of life somehow struck a chord with billions of people throughout the world, and that person is Jesus.

It's relatively easy in today's technologically advanced and well-connected world for someone to become a worldwide influence, even in a matter of minutes. The popularity of social media platforms is ever increasing with many becoming addicted. Hunger for more entertainment encourages modern-day influencers to create endless content for their fans to feast on, attracting more clicks, likes and views. So how did Jesus do it? Well, Jesus lived at just the right time in history, in fact, the era he lived in was the first time the world was truly connected. When I say the world, I'm referring to the known world at that time, which included modern-day Northern Africa, Asia Minor, Europe and the Middle East. Upheavals and conflicts were constant prior to Jesus' birth. By the time he was born, the world was in relative peace, called, *Pax Romana*, the peace which existed between nationalities and ethnic groups within the Roman Empire. The Romans had ruled from approximately 27 BC and were a military powerhouse. They hardly had any rivals that could match their might and there was no threat to the Empire in the foreseeable future. That meant peace would reign for decades ahead so that Jesus' message and influence would be unhindered from conflicts and wars. Prior to the Roman Empire taking control, a common language was introduced as a result of the conquests of Alexander the Great. This had spread throughout the known world. That language was Greek, also known as *trade Greek*, which was systematically used to make communication possible between people who did not share a native language or dialect. That meant everyone, no matter where they were from within the Empire, could communicate with each other. This common language remained in use throughout Jesus' life. Another factor of the well-connected landscape at that time was the travel from place to place and town to town. This was made easier by the

Roman's relentless desire for expansion. Always looking for ways to better improve the movement of goods, food and soldiers, they built roads throughout the Empire. This meant Jesus and his followers could travel from place to place, on foot, to communicate their message. It's quite amazing when you think about it. That at just the right time of Jesus' birth, all these aspects were in place; peace, a common language and infrastructure. Not just for his reach within society but for his followers to continue the teachings of Jesus well after his death.

Today, and throughout history, there is confusion about what Jesus and his disciples taught. Followers of Jesus should mirror the life of Jesus, but in many instances, they aren't the best examples of Jesus' teachings and way of life. So what is the truth about Jesus and how can we know for certain what Jesus actually taught and said? There are eyewitness accounts as recorded in the Gospels of Matthew, Mark, Luke and John in the New Testament of the Bible. But even after reading these texts, some may still be unsure of what Jesus and his followers meant. The Bible must be read in context and mustn't be read like a magazine. There are some texts easy enough to understand while other texts contain deep insight that is better understood with further research.

There is misunderstanding and confusion surrounding the meaning of specific terms and words. These can be difficult to articulate in English from the original language the Bible was written in. The original biblical texts were written in Greek, Hebrew and Aramaic. When transposed to English, there are certain phrases and words that get lost in translation. An example would be the English word, *love*. Love is the only word in English we have for *love*. However, in the Greek language, there are four main definitions for the word, *love*; *Eros*, which means romantic love; *Philia*, which means brotherly or friendship love; *Storge*, which means parental love, and *Agape,* which means unconditional *God-like* love. This is where an in-depth understanding of the biblical texts is helpful as the deeper meaning can be overlooked.

The reason I've written this book is to shed the light of Jesus' teachings and clarify certain passages. I've chosen several topics that relate to our world today as much as it did 2000 years ago. I'll focus on the life of Jesus and his teachings surrounding these topics. I'll back them up with biblical New Testament texts written by the eyewitnesses of Jesus, or those who had close fellowship with an eyewitness. How can we be certain what was written 2000 years ago is accurate, you may ask? Well, the New Testament texts were well preserved. They have been copied generation after generation since the first century. As of today, we have over 5000 Greek manuscripts, and well over 20,000 if you consider other languages with more copies being found as time goes on. These copies match with almost precise accuracy. The parts that are erroneous are incredibly minute and relate to spelling and grammatical differences which most likely occurred when the scribes got a little lazy-eyed. Not one error impacts the main message of Jesus' teachings in any way. This means the Bible that we have today is what was written over 2000 years ago. So regardless of your opinion of the text's divine inspiration, the evidence leans heavily toward the New Testament being a precise historical narrative account, especially of Jesus' life and teachings.

Despite popular belief, the Bible was not put together by the Catholic Church, Emperor Constantine, or by a group of men that convened at the Council of Nicaea. If anything, the Council of Nicaea just, *rubber-stamped*, what was already considered the Bible. The biblical texts existed well before any Christian religious institution began. The books that we have in the Bible today are what was known and accepted as the authoritative holy texts in the known world at that time. The biblical texts were so well known they acted as a safeguard against anyone adding or subtracting to it, which would have been addressed and extinguished at the time. The Gospels and New Testament books were written within decades after Jesus' death. Not hundreds of years as is commonly assumed. Compare this with other ancient documents throughout history and nothing comes so close to the time of the writings and the person's death. The fact that the Gospels were written so close to the life of Jesus gives credibility to the accuracy of the eyewitness accounts, as most of the eyewitnesses were still alive to affirm their accounts (1 Corinthians 15:5–7). These are just some pieces of evidence that lead to the credibility of the biblical texts. There are many comprehensive books that delve into the evidence and reliability of the biblical texts.

Another question that is raised is how can we be certain Jesus existed? The simple answer to that is, he absolutely existed. More will be said about this in the first chapter, *Who Is Jesus*.

For the record, I do believe that Jesus is the Messiah, the Son of God that gave his life for the sins of the world. Considering that the evidence is stacked towards Jesus' existence, you too will have to wrestle with who Jesus is. The options are few when considering who Jesus is. He is either the Lord, a fraudster or a madman. The one thing he can't be is a good teacher because the biblical texts state that he claimed Lordship; that he claimed to be the Son of God. If you don't accept his claims as Lordship, then you are essentially labelling him a liar and an impostor, and so he can't be 'good'.

Many will say that they accept some quotes of the Bible and not all, like accepting Jesus' teaching but excluding his claims as Lord and Messiah. But to cherry-pick the texts you like, and disregard the texts you don't like is simply based on a personal bias. To do such a thing would be intellectually dishonest, that's regardless of what side of the fence you sit on. You either accept all biblical texts or reject all of them. It can't be partially true. If you would like to delve into the evidence supporting the biblical texts and the person of Jesus, his claims and his life. I recommend these books; *The Case for Christ by Lee Strobel* and *Cold-Case Christianity by J. Warner Wallace*.

Jesus is both divine and human. I know this can be a struggle for our finite minds to grasp. I elaborate on this a little in the following chapter. This book focuses on the man, Jesus, and his humanity. What I've written isn't a comprehensive examination of the life and teachings of Jesus. Rather, I give an insight into certain biblical texts and moments in Jesus' life surrounding the topical chapters; to clarify and explain the deeper meaning of his life and teachings in what might otherwise be overlooked. I'll also be looking at the legacy he left for his followers and the world. The chapters in this book cover topics that confront us in our society today.

For those familiar with the Bible, you will notice I didn't take any textual references from the Old Testament. This is because Jesus didn't live in that time. Although there are prophetic references to Jesus, his life and teaching begin and continue throughout the New Testament. Some may point out certain texts from the Old Testament relating to some of the topics I've written about. But the Old Testament is a totally different type of literature that requires it to be understood on its own. In brief, the Old Testament is a historical account of the people of Israel and events of that time. The customs, and what some might call obscure guidelines, were written for the Theocracy of Israel. Meant for a certain time, culture and people groups, who were extremely susceptible to outside influences that easily led them astray. To explain the questionable biblical texts from the Old Testament would require a whole other book written on those topics. That's not what this book is about, it's about focusing on the life and teachings of Jesus, which is where followers of Jesus, Christians, get their morality and guidance from.

Some might say that the God of the Old Testament comes across as angry and mean. That this contradicts the God of the New Testament who comes across as more loving as revealed through Jesus. This is not true. Granted, God does seem to dish out more judgment in the Old Testament, however, he is actually very loving, compassionate and patient with the people. The way God treated people in the Old Testament times is different from the New Testament times. This is because God responds to the level of humanity's development of faith. As recorded in the Old Testament, the people, especially those that claimed to be followers of God, were so easily led away into some atrocious acts of evil like child sacrifice. By New Testament times, the people weren't so easily led astray. For instance, a teacher teaching a child from the years five to 16, won't apply the same level of instruction year after year. Rather, as the child grows in knowledge and understanding, more in-depth knowledge will be applied.

The social environment Jesus lived in was heavily patriarchal and full of sexism. To be honest, it would have been a terrible time to be a woman. Racism was intense between ethnicities and religious groups. Inequality based on wealth and ability. A misguided moral society that taught if you do 'good' to me, I'll do 'good' to you. A love for others that extended only as far as likeness. If you are like me and my kind, culture and belief, then I accept and love you. Money ruled society and corrupted the political and religious ruling elites. Religion became a tool to control the masses, a belief and faith void of heart and compassion. A time of tense political movements, wanting control of people and land. You know, as I'm writing this, it sounds like I'm not just writing about the social environment over 2000 years ago, but our world today! Jesus entered the scene for such a time as this. To change hearts and minds; to create better societies and to create a better world. Unfortunately, Jesus' way of life is largely overlooked. The mistreatment of others, conflicts, gender inequality and wars continue to rage on. In some areas, they are only increasing as time goes by. No matter your belief or none, if you want to know with more certainty what Jesus has to say about such topics, read on.

This book is meant to be read with a bible on hand if you wish to look up the biblical stories and references that I haven't quoted in this book. The version I used is the NIV (New International Version). If you don't have a physical Bible, you can access it online for free at; *https://www.biblegateway.com/* alternatively you can download the Bible app for free by typing 'bible' in the App Store or via the website; https://www.bible.com/app.

Before I finish this introduction, I'd like to tell you a true story to give you an idea of the influence that Jesus has on the world. The story of, the *Christmas Truce*, happened during World War I. In the ravages of arguably the most horrific wars the world has ever seen, labelled, *the war to end all wars*, Jesus brought peace between enemies even if only for a few days. In 1914, during World War I, a large section of the Western Front fell silent for several days. About 100,000 soldiers laid down their weapons, came out of their trenches and peaceably spent Christmas together. Enemies that were just trying to eliminate each other came together in peace, exchanging gifts; whatever items they had on them at the time. Even showing photographs of their families to each other. They sang Christmas Carols together, decorated their surroundings and trenches, and shared Christmas greetings. It's amazing how the birth of a baby over 1900 years prior, could affect the hearts of so many battle-hardened soldiers that have no doubt become desensitised due to the brutality of the war. It's been called a miracle, a rare moment of peace in a horrendous war that ended up taking over 15 million lives. It's reasonable to see that Jesus has a tremendous influence on the world, even from the very start of his life on earth.

Who Is Jesus

Very few historians, Christian or not, would deny the existence of Jesus. The vast majority will agree he was a real person that lived around 2000 years ago in modern-day Israel/Palestine. Apart from the biblical texts of Jesus' life, there are several non-biblical sources that confirm the existence of Jesus. Two notable textual sources are the writings of the Jewish historian, *Josephus*, and the Roman historian, *Tacitus*. They weren't followers of Jesus yet wrote about him. I've done my own research on this topic and the evidence of Jesus' existence is overwhelming. But don't take it from me; I would implore you to do your own research.

Greater debate surrounds his incredible claims about being the Son of God, his miracles, death and resurrection. Again, if interested, I would suggest further research. To me, the historical, scientific, archaeological, psychological and manuscript evidence points to the trustworthiness of the Gospel accounts of Jesus' life, death and resurrection. The two books I mentioned in the introduction are a good start if you would like to delve further. It's worth mentioning that although both authors are followers of Jesus; when they began their investigations, they were staunch Atheists.

Jesus also claimed to be God in human form (John 10:30). You might ask, 'How does that work? How can he be God and the Son of God?' This is a mystery indeed. He wouldn't be God if we could grasp everything about him. I wrote another book called, *Our Father,* where I delve deeper into the topic of God the father and God the Son. Of course, there are other, more in-depth resources out there too. Jesus claimed to live out the heart of God (John 5:19). Jesus spoke and lived the very nature of God, which is why you will notice I interchange between Jesus and God throughout this book.

An interesting fact pointing to the credibility of Jesus' resurrection is Jesus doesn't have a grave. Central figures of other religions have gravesites, but Jesus doesn't. Being the revered figure he was, even by the few followers that remained, there would be a burial site that would almost be impossible to have kept hidden, and would certainly be known about today. If the overwhelming evidence is that Jesus existed, and most historians agree with this, then it leads to the credibility of the eyewitness's claim of Jesus' resurrection as recorded in the Gospels. But no matter your belief about Jesus, there's no question he taught some amazing things and lived an incredible life that was counter-cultural in many ways, even by today's standards. So let's look into his life a little deeper to see who Jesus really is.

One man, Jesus, born over 2000 years ago is the most recognised person in history. Online algorithm searches show that Jesus is constantly the number one most looked up and recognised person in the world, way ahead of any other major historical or religious figure. Apart from being the central figure of Christianity, Jesus is a major figure within the other monotheistic faiths. He is also acknowledged among Eastern faith groups, and over 90% of non-believers know who Jesus is. No matter how much or how little people know about him, his name is known all over the world. There are many famous and infamous figures throughout history but if you look at why these historical figures are well known, there is a stark contrast. They led great conquests, defeated armies, achieved incredible feats, and wielded incredible power and fortune. While Jesus was just a common guy, a tradesman who was crucified on a Roman cross, what's to ride home about that? Yet his legacy has outlasted the greatest kingdoms that have ever existed. The most powerful world leaders and aristocrats that have ever lived don't come close to the type of influence Jesus has made in this world.

So what makes Jesus the most well-known person in the world? Could it be his great moral and ethical teachings, like nothing that was heard or has ever been heard? Could it be his many miracles of healing the sick and bringing people back to life? Is it the declaration that he died for all of humanity's sins so that we can be reconciled to God? Is it the outstanding claim that he rose to life again, seen by many witnesses, most of whom were persecuted and put to death because of their claim that they saw him alive after the crucifixion? People are not likely to die for what they know to be a lie.

Quite frankly, when you line Jesus up against other historical figures, his worldly achievements make him a no-name really, miracles aside. Think about it, there's no record of Jesus' day of birth, yet the calendar in the western world is linked to the approximate start of his life on earth. Though a miraculous conception, he came into the world by birth like everybody else, although a stable would not have been the first choice of any mother to deliver her child. The four

Gospels detailing Jesus' life have been translated into a plethora of languages, somewhere between 1500 and 2000. More than any other manuscript or book in existence and more languages are being added to that list as time goes by. He is the dominant figure in the most purchased book of all time and ironically the most stolen book of all time. He didn't author a book or leave behind great works of literature and yet he is the subject of countless books, more than anyone else in history. He inspires songs, movies and many other art forms, yet Jesus himself didn't paint a masterpiece or compose a song. He didn't lead a political movement, yet billions of people throughout generations have placed Jesus as the leader of their lives. He didn't lead a rebellion or an army; he didn't conquer a single inch of land, yet in every generation, he has had more followers than the entire world's armies combined. Millions have laid down their lives for him. Every year, tens of thousands are put to death because of their faith in Jesus. Hundreds of millions are being oppressed in some form because of their belief in him. Christians are the most persecuted people group in the world. He didn't travel to distant lands; in fact, he stayed within a relatively small area, yet his influence has reached every nation and corner of the globe. Jesus has been the most followed person in the world since the first century by every generation to date. He doesn't hold a degree or academic achievement. He was your average Jewish schoolboy that would have fulfilled the standard education requirement at the time. Yet his life and teachings are intensely spoken about and debated in educational institutions and conferences around the world.

Jesus spent just three years publicly teaching, he spoke to multitudes but mostly to small groups of people, not eighty

17

thousand seat coliseums. He wasn't rich or powerful nor did he hold any influential sway. Instead, he was quite the opposite, a poor and relatively unknown citizen under the tyrannical Roman Government and Jewish religious hierarchy. He earned an honest living by following his dad's trade, a carpenter. He didn't have a child, no heir to carry on his cause. His main followers were a bunch of misfits really, cowards, some said to be unlearned and not all that eloquent (Acts 4:13). Most of the people and religious leaders rejected him and even his own family had their doubts about him (Mark 3:21).

Jesus died a criminal's death, which was an embarrassment and a disgrace for anyone within the Jewish community at that time. And apart from a few close followers and family, all else had disregarded him as a blasphemer and charlatan that deserved to be executed. Relatively unknown outside of the country he lived in, yet millions in the world study and read his words daily. Jesus and his teachings are topics of passionate debates like no other, billions adore him, and millions abhor him. His life was intensely and ruthlessly scrutinised through the ages by the most respected and revered philosophers and historians. Whether some like to admit it or not, democratic nations are built on the foundations of Jesus' teachings. Jesus is the reason we celebrate Christmas and Easter, although Santa and the Easter Bunny are the lead figures in today's secular culture. It can't be denied that these significant days acknowledged around the world are derived from the birth, death and resurrection of Jesus.

No matter which way you look at it, there is no dispute that this man, Jesus, from the backwater town of Nazareth, is the most controversial, divisive, praised and worshipped,

18

mocked and ridiculed, admired, shunned, famous, rejected, provoking, honoured, dishonoured, most censored, most glorified, mimicked, mistaken, commended, condemned, recited, loved, hated, influential and significant person in all of human history, and will be for generations to come.

Women

This chapter is the longest and for good reason. It's a major issue in our world today and I'm sure most, if not all, would have the topic of gender equality at the top of the list of things that need addressing in our society and around the world. It sure was high on Jesus' priority list. Women are made by God, they have dignity and value, and they are his precious daughters. There are many teachings and references that back this up, hence the long chapter. There is confusion and misquoting of New Testament texts that seem to demean women. These questionable texts make reference to how women should behave and their roles as wives, but there is a deeper meaning to these passages than just taking the words at face value. We will look at these instances in this chapter. There should be no confusion though about Jesus' teaching and treatment of women. He was a champion for women's rights. He broke down the walls of misogyny in what was an unbearably hostile environment for women. If you were to compare Jesus' teachings with other religious faiths or their founders, there is no comparison. Jesus treated women with dignity and worth, and he affirmed women's rights like no other.

The Declarations

Jesus' declarations of the Messiahship and the first declared sighting of his resurrection were both first witnessed by women. This is quite significant considering that a woman's testimony was not valid in a court of law at that time in history, as women were considered intellectually inferior. It's been suggested that there were traditional sayings at the time, '*Blessed is the man that has sons instead of daughters*', and, '*let the word of God be destroyed rather than taught to women*'. Ouch! Talk about degrading women. As you can see, a woman's worth was not highly regarded according to the ruling religious and governing establishments. It's probably the reason why Peter, a disciple of Jesus who grew up with this type of cultural bias, ran to the tomb to see for himself if Jesus had indeed risen from the dead. Even though Mary and the other women told him that they had seen Jesus alive. It reads, '*But they did not believe the women, because their words seemed to them like nonsense*' (Luke 24:11). Peter and the other disciples had the deeply held cultural belief that a woman's word can't be trusted. I'm sure Jesus intended for women to be the first witnesses to his resurrection as an example for the disciples. To show that Jesus can and will use anyone, including women to spread the message, and to break down the prejudice against women. Let's look into these declarations Jesus made to these women. Firstly, we have the woman at the well, you can read the whole story in full in the Gospel of John (chapter 4, vv. 1–42). The story of Jesus' conversation with the woman at the well is the longest recorded conversation in the Bible. Men didn't typically speak with women unless they were family, that's probably why the disciples were surprised to find Jesus talking with a woman (v. 27). What we ascertain from this woman is that she has been married five times and the man she was living with wasn't her husband. At the start of the story, it gives us the time of day, it was about noon. This likely meant she was a social outcast and rejected by the other women in her village because of her many marriages. Back then, women travelled in groups to fetch water because of safety in numbers and to socialise. They would go during the cooler times of the day like dusk or dawn, rather than midday when it's hottest. She probably preferred to avoid travelling with such groups, to avoid their gossip and finger-pointing. It was culturally acceptable for a man to be married five times but not a woman. She was thrown into society's scrapheap. But Jesus saw the true value of this woman despite the cultural rejection because of her gender. He has a deep conversation with her about faith and worship. After the woman said, '*I know that Messiah is coming*' (v. 25), Jesus responded, '*I am he, the one speaking to you*' (v. 26). This person, a woman, whom society has deemed unreliable. Useless, apart from menial tasks and homely duties that societal norms have imposed on her, was the first person to have been given the greatest insight and knowledge of Jesus being the prophesied Messiah, from the Messiah himself. Till that point, Jesus did not disclose his true identity to anyone, not even the disciples. She was the first person to have received the truth about Jesus' true identity. Not only was this woman a social outcast because of her gender, she was a moral outcast because of her many failed marriages, but Jesus found her worthy of instruction and broke down a significant societal barrier.

The second declaration is the first appearance of Jesus' resurrection. The resurrection is the integral moment of the

Christian faith. In fact, the Christian faith hinges on that moment. Without the resurrection, the Christian faith is useless. The Apostle Paul made a telling statement, '*If Christ has not been raised, your faith is futile*' (1 Corinthians 15:17). The resurrection of Jesus is undoubtedly the foundation stone of the Christian faith. So it's imperative that the first witnesses to the most important moment of the Christian faith were reliable and worthy of witnessing to others. The story of the first appearance after Jesus' resurrection can be read in full in the Gospel of Matthew (chapter 28, vv. 1–10). It is incredibly significant that Jesus appeared as the resurrected Messiah first and foremost to women. This instance of the first resurrection appearance is a significant declaration. In a society where women are seen as inferior and unintelligent; their words can't be taken seriously or trusted to testify in court. Jesus smashes all the negative preconceived notions about women. In the most defining moment of the Christian faith, the moment that changed the course of the world, Jesus first appeared to women. Think about it, if he wanted to, Jesus could have first appeared to his male disciples, after all, they were his right-hand men for most of his ministerial life. But he didn't. I believe this is Jesus' way of showing the disciples that if Jesus held women with such high regard, they should too. He wanted to teach them that women are worthy to be taught and to preach and teach his message and that women had an integral part to play within the church.

It's interesting to note that, to be a Christian, one must believe that Jesus is the resurrected Messiah. These women were the first witnesses to the resurrection and had believed because they obeyed Jesus' request to tell the other disciples what they had seen (vv. 9–11). Truth is, these women were

23

the very first people to have proclaimed the resurrected Messiah. Therefore making them the very first Christians that had ever existed. The first and foremost pioneers of the Christian faith, the *foremothers of the Christian faith*.

Protection

Jesus introduced many protections for women at a time when they were treated as possessions and objects. In what was a male-dominated society, women hardly had any rights in public. They were afforded a few more rights within the home. Women were controlled by a male figure all their life from father to husband to son and were pretty much treated as slaves with a little more rights than actual slaves. A woman could not seek a divorce from her husband but a husband can divorce his wife for any reason, something as trivial as not being able to make him a satisfactory dinner. All he had to do was give her a certificate of divorce and send her on her way. In essence, anything the woman did wrong in her husband's eyes was her fault, and he had every right to leave her according to the customs and laws as designed by men. It was socially acceptable for men, married or not, to have intimate relations with many women. It was expected that women have intimate relations with their husbands only, otherwise, they would be severely punished. According to the culture, a wife is guilty of adultery against her husband by having an affair with another man (married or not). However, if a husband had an affair with another married woman, he is guilty of adultery against that woman's husband and is not guilty of adultery against his own wife.

Due to the poor treatment of women and the fact that girls were married-off by their male relatives, they were heavily reliant upon men taking care of them. If there was no husband, the caretaker role would fall to the father or another male relative. If there was no man to take care of the woman, she would most likely be poverty-stricken and homeless. So Jesus made sure that women would be taken care of and not easily discarded, just because the husband felt like it. Jesus elevated the status of women and wives. In the Gospel of Mark, Jesus puts the onus on the men, saying, '*Anyone who divorces his wife and marries another woman commits adultery against her*' (emphasis added), (Mark 10:11). Jesus was contradicting the cultural status quo. Making it an equal playing field. Men are not above women, and they can't get away with such mistreatment. While on the topic of adultery, Jesus taught, '*Anyone who looks at a woman lustfully has already committed adultery with her in his heart*' (Matthew 5:28). Again, this puts the onus on the man; that looking at a woman with lustful intent is a violation against women, she is more than an object. In effect, Jesus was saying that if the man took a woman by force because he couldn't control himself, he is to blame, not the woman. In a society where it was acceptable to mistreat women if they didn't act or dress appropriately, Jesus made it clear that the fault lies with the one who commits the offence. Basically saying that each person is responsible for their own actions. Especially in a society and culture where men got away with such flagrant mistreatment of women. Jesus set out to change the attitudes of men, more specifically husbands, to be faithful to their wives.

A great example of Jesus' protection of women, is the story of the woman that was caught in the act of adultery. This story can be read in the Gospel of John (chapter 8, vv. 3–11). Here we read about a woman that was brought to Jesus by the religious leaders and teachers of the law, they were all men. They asked Jesus what he thought about stoning the woman since that is what the law allows for the offence of adultery (vv. 4–5). Notice that she was *caught in the act*, meaning the man was there also but they let him off the hook and apprehended the woman only. It's possible the religious leaders orchestrated the event. Paying a man to trap an unsuspecting woman. To use her like bait to entrap Jesus, knowing full well that she would most likely be stoned to death simply because they wanted to prove a point. Jesus stood up for the woman with a brilliant response, saving her from certain death. Unlike those religious hypocrites that sought to punish the woman because of her gender, Jesus saw the intrinsic value of her life regardless of her gender.

Another example of Jesus' care and protection for women was at his most excruciating and agonising moment. While Jesus was on the cross being crucified, just before his last few breaths, he made sure his mother was taken care of (John 19:26–27). Jesus said to his mother, '*Here is your son*', speaking of the disciple next to her (most likely the only male disciple there at his crucifixion). He then said to the disciple, '*Here is your mother*'. From that moment on, that disciple took care of Jesus' mother as his own. Jesus wasn't suggesting that women are helpless and need a man to take care of them, rather he understood the cultural restrictions placed on women at the time. As mentioned a few paragraphs ago, if Jesus's mother had no male figure to look after her, she most likely would be homeless.

When you read the story of Jesus' journey to the cross, it was women who are prominent throughout this event. They certainly mourned the most and the majority weren't related to Jesus. They loved him deeply, not just for who he was but for how he treated them. He was a great loss for the women, most likely being the only male public figure that treated them as equals, with dignity and respect. He spoke up for the women when no one else would in such a patriarchal society.

Teaching

A woman had no right to teach or to be taught. However, if a woman was fortunate enough to grow up in a wealthy or prestigious family, she may have had her way. The vast majority of women were uneducated, not even being able to read. Unfortunately, this extended to religious society. Women had their own section on the temple grounds and they could only observe the religious ceremonies, not participate. Women were not to be spoken to, not to be educated in the religious law apart from the basics. A woman's place was to walk behind her husband. Women could certainly not be students or disciples of any religious teacher, let alone travel with them. Jesus changed all that. He openly taught, talked to and allowed women as followers. Never once did he discourage or degrade women. When you read the Gospels, it becomes clear that Jesus respected women highly and always had in mind to include women in the work he commissioned to his followers.

In the Gospel of Luke (chapter 10, vv. 38–42), we read about how Jesus went to the home of two sisters, Martha and Mary. Jesus was teaching and Mary sat at the feet of Jesus, the position and place of a male student, while Martha was distracted by preparations. Martha told Jesus to tell her sister to help her, but Jesus responded, '*Mary has chosen what is better, and it will not be taken away from her*' (v. 42). Firstly, I just want to point out that Jesus wasn't suggesting that Martha's attempt to take care of her guests wasn't important. By the sound of it, she was going overboard and was overly concerned to the point of being distracted (v. 40). Another way to look at it is that Martha succumbed to the role society allotted to her, while Mary chose to break away from society's mould and sit by Jesus' feet to learn. Martha, in speaking out, probably thought that since Jesus was a teacher, he would be on her side. That Mary's role, as a woman, was not to learn by Jesus' feet, but rather to slave away in the kitchen. Jesus loved the fact that Mary was by his feet, wanting to learn from him. There is no suggestion whatsoever that Mary should not have been there, that she should not be learning; or to give up her place to a male student. Rather, Jesus affirmed Mary's choice to learn. That she has a mind and is worthy of religious instruction, and that her desire to learn will not be taken away from her. This was incredibly counter-cultural considering that the religious leaders of that time taught and discipled men only.

We read in John 20 (v. 16), how Mary Magdalene exclaimed, *Rabboni*, which means teacher, an indication that she too was a student of Jesus. And Jesus even taught about women by including them in his parables and stories, like the parable of the lost coin (Luke 15:8–10); the two women grinding at the mill (Luke 17:35); and the persistent widow (Luke 18:1–8).

How Did Jesus Treat Women?

Jesus treated women very differently than how society dictated. He paved the way for his followers, especially his disciples, about how women should be treated. Apart from female family members, men would not converse with women unless it was absolutely necessary. Jesus, on the other hand, did speak with women. As mentioned earlier, he taught women and allowed them to be his followers, something that was unthinkable for a religious teacher. Women knew that religious leaders would not allow women students or followers. However, the women were drawn to Jesus. Throughout his life, he showed gentleness and respect, and the women felt comfortable enough to assume he would be accepting of their presence and following. One example would have been when he saved the woman from being stoned (John 8:3–11). He showed an incredible amount of care and respect for this woman who was otherwise labelled as unclean and unworthy by the rest of society. No doubt the women bystanders would have been taken aback by Jesus' stance to save this woman from certain death. As women constantly communed and met together, word would have spread within the female groups about Jesus' care and respect for women.

Another illustration of Jesus' respect for women is the story about Jesus healing a woman who had suffered a sickness for twelve years (Mark 5:24–34). This woman was a social pariah, deemed unclean by society. Here we read the only scripturally documented term of endearment uttered by Jesus, and it was said to this woman. A woman who was an outcast because of her debilitating illness. According to the culture, she was untouchable because of her constant bleeding *and* she was a woman, which made her doubly cursed. She had spent all she had on trying to cure her illness and was most likely homeless. No one, not even her own family would accept her because the religious rules of the day declared her unclean. Anyone who came in contact with her would also be unclean. If she had been married, she was divorced. Excommunicated from community and religious life. She truly was on the bottom rung of society. She suffered greatly, not just from the physical pain but the emotional pain of being unloved; not having heard any type of endearing words for the past twelve years. She was more likely to have been taunted and teased. But Jesus did not shoo her away, in fact, he recognised her faith. He made sure that she knew that he acknowledged her (vv. 31–32). As Jesus looked around for this person of great faith, the woman fell at Jesus' feet thinking that she had done something wrong and would be condemned by Jesus. Instead, he said quite the opposite. He praised her faith, granted peace upon her and something that strikingly stands out, he called her, *Daughter*. This would have been the first time in twelve years she would have heard an endearing term. Jesus healed her physical pain, but he also healed her emotional pain. By calling her daughter, he removed any self-doubt and instilled a sense of dignity and value; that if no one else saw her as precious, he did. He restored her socially too, by affirming his acceptance of her in front of the large crowd.

Mary Magdalene

Considering the New Testament Gospels were written approximately 2000 years ago in a male-dominated society, there is a fair amount of attention given to Mary Magdalene.

She is mentioned about 14 times by name within all four Gospel accounts which is more than most of the male disciples. We don't know much about her besides that she was healed by Jesus from evil spirits and diseases (Luke 8:2), which meant she was unclean and an outcast. She travelled with Jesus wherever he went as a follower and supporter. She was there at the most defining moments of Jesus' life, death and resurrection. It's suggested she was a very independent woman because women at that time were associated with a male figure of their family. For instance, she wasn't called, *Mary, daughter of John*. This could've meant she shed the tag of any male authority on her life and instead was known as Mary Magdalene (Magdalene being the name of a town). So it's quite significant she chose to be a follower of Jesus, a male teacher. Apart from Jesus healing her, she must have seen something different in him, most likely the way he treated women. She was also part of an integrated support group of women that sustained Jesus' ministry out of their own means (Luke 8:3).

Women's Importance in the Church

Women didn't have significant roles in religious life for several reasons. They were mostly uneducated, seen as unclean because of natural bodily functions, unwise and could not be trusted. But Jesus publicly included women when he taught them and never once turned them away. This was counter-cultural of the time, especially amongst the religious elite. We see many insights of the role of women in Jesus's life throughout the Gospels and New Testament letters.

One of the very first people to proclaim Jesus as the Messiah was Anna, a prophet who resided in the temple (Luke 2:36–38). The only person recorded in scripture to have washed Jesus' feet and anointed his head, as an act of reverence and worship, was a woman (Matthew 26:6–13). Jesus affirms her act of worship by saying, '*She has done a beautiful thing to me*' (v. 10). '*Wherever the gospel is preached throughout the world, what she has done will also be told in memory of her*' (v. 13). Out of all the acts of reverence shown to Jesus, he highly regarded this woman's act of worship and devotion that it would forever be recorded in memory of *her*. Jesus didn't condemn her act even though she broke some cultural customs of that time. Approaching Jesus at the table where he ate; women and men ate at separate tables. She let her hair down in public; this was deemed an act of intimacy between husband and wife. She wiped his feet with her hair in view of everyone; a very intimate and forbidden act indeed. Jesus accepted her act of devotion and worship, but he also defended it when the disciples spoke out against her (v. 10).

The Samaritan woman at the well whom Jesus spoke to. She went back to her village and told them about Jesus. They came to see Jesus and believed him to be the Saviour because of this woman's proclamation (John 4:39–42), she helped grow the church by her witness. In the Gospel of Luke (chapter 8, vv. 2–3), we read about a group of women that followed Jesus in his ministry as he and his disciples travelled. It mentions the women were supporting them out of their own means. These women physically and financially sustained the very beginnings of the early church. They were active and significant members of the church's growth in its early days.

If it wasn't for their assistance and support, Jesus' message may not have had as great a reach as it did. Jesus didn't ignore them or stop them from helping. He accepted and valued their role in assisting his ministry, and these women were from various backgrounds and social statuses. Mary Magdalene was an outcast and deemed unclean. Joanna was the wife of Chuza, who was the manager of Herod's household, a woman of influence and affluence. The assistance of women is also mentioned in the Gospel of Mark (chapter 15, vv. 40–41), these women followed Jesus and cared for his needs. It states there were *many* women, and some were mentioned by name.

When you read the Gospels, you will see that women were a part of some pretty significant moments in Jesus' life. It was a girl, Mary, that was given the first announcement of Jesus' birth (Luke 1:26–33). It was a woman that Jesus spoke the only recorded term of endearment to (Mark 5:34). It was a woman that Jesus honours for her great act of devotion, that it would forever be recorded in her memory (Matthew 26:13). It was a woman who told her towns' people about the Messiah Jesus; they all believed because of *her* testimony (John 4:39–42). It was women that provided their own means to support and uphold the early church (Mark 15:40–41). It was predominantly women that stayed and kept a vigil as Jesus died an excruciating death on the cross (John 19:25), while the men stayed away in fear. It was women that prepared the spices for embalmment and woke early to go to the tomb to prepare Jesus' body for burial (Luke 24:1). It was women that the angels first appeared to, to announce the resurrection of Jesus (Matthew 28:5–6). It was women who first saw Jesus risen from the dead (Matthew 28:8–9). It was women that first proclaimed the resurrected Jesus to others, Jesus personally commissioned the women to do so (Matthew 28:10). It was women that first remembered the words that Jesus spoke, about being crucified and rising again on the third day (Luke 24:5–8). It was women who first believed and understood the resurrection, even before the male disciples did (Luke 24:9–11). There is no question that women have an integral and equal, if not more important, part to play within the global Christian church. God made sure there was more than enough evidence in the biblical texts to support their involvement and importance.

We'll now look at the other New Testament books that follow the Gospels. Here, the followers of Jesus carry on the teachings of Jesus after his resurrection. We continue to see the importance of women's role within the church. The book of Acts notes the early beginnings of the Christian movement. It's noted (Acts 1:14), that the men were together with the women in the upper room. The first signs of worship equality. The cultural norm expected men and women to gather and worship separately. Reading on in Acts (chapter 2), we read how the Holy Spirit comes upon all of them, this includes the women. This is the Holy Spirit's confirmation that women are part of the church and have an equal and integral role. In Acts 9:36, we read of a woman in the faith, named Tabitha, being referred to as a disciple in a society known for male discipleship only. In Acts 16:13, we see how some of the men who were spreading the word came to Philippi and began to speak to the women who had gathered there. Direct teaching to women was not customary. Continue reading and we see how Lydia, a wealthy business woman became a believer and offered her house to the followers of the faith. Lydia, being the first recorded believer in Europe made her house a church

34

where people of the faith met (Acts 16:40). In effect, Lydia formed the very first church building in Europe. Some historians suggest Lydia was the first European convert; that her conversion was a significant moment for the church and Western civilization. Again in the book of Acts 18:26, we read that Priscilla and her husband Aquila taught and explained the way of God to Apollos, a man. Note that Priscilla was mentioned first in the text, she was a prominent figure in the church at the time, even more so than her husband. She is mentioned several times in the texts, and in most instances, she is mentioned before her husband.

In Paul's personal greetings to the church in Romans 16:1–15, most of the people he mentions by name are women. This would have been unheard of at that time, to give women such a prominent standing among men, and he lauds their role in the church. He doesn't disapprove of their involvement in the church, in fact, he praises them and acknowledges them as sisters and co-workers in the faith. The first person he commends is Phoebe. Tradition states she most likely carried the letter of *Romans*, from Paul to the church in Rome. Because of her, we have the book of Romans as we know it in the Bible. Paul calls her a deacon of the church (v. 1), this term was used for someone who held office, a minister of the early church. He mentions, *Junia*, who he said is outstanding among the apostles (v. 7). Paul also mentions, *Nympia*, running another church in her house (Colossians 4:15). In the early days of the Christian church, the people often met in homes because there weren't proper church buildings yet. Paul speaks favourably of the church run by Nympia, sending his greeting, and showing his approval for women running churches.

These are just a few examples in scripture of the roles that women had in the early church. You will see a lot more affirming references if you read the New Testament writings for yourself. These accounts aren't recorded by accident, they are there for a reason. To confirm and declare the importance of women in the church. Their proclamation, their worship and devotion, their presence, teaching, and running of churches, and their every involvement is crucial to the church and should be recognised as such.

Questionable Scriptures in The New Testament

Considering the scriptural evidence of Jesus' positive treatment and affirmation of women, there are questions about some of the New Testament writings by Jesus' followers. At face value they scream misogyny, however, there is a deeper meaning to these scriptures and they must be read in context. The Apostle Paul, who made these remarks is one of the greatest supporters of Jesus' teaching, so why would he write what seems to be demoralising statements?

I also want women to dress modestly, with decency and propriety, adorning themselves, not with elaborate hairstyles or gold or pearls or expensive clothes, but with good deeds, appropriate for women who profess to worship God. A woman should learn in quietness and full submission. I do not permit a woman to teach or have authority over a man; she must be quiet. 1 Timothy 2:9–12.

Women should remain silent in the churches. They are not allowed to speak but must be in submission, as the law says.

If they want to inquire about something, they should ask their own husbands at home; for it is disgraceful for a woman to speak in church. 1 Corinthians 14:34–35.

These remarks contradict what Jesus taught and how he treated women. So why would the Apostle Paul say such things, especially after the examples I've noted about his support for women in church and ministry? Paul, who wrote these letters, addressed them to certain people and people groups; addressing specific circumstances. He was instructing the new Christian believers living in a stubborn culture, entrenched in their mistreatment of women. To have come out a full blast in condemnation of the poor treatment of women, would have ruined any chance of the Christian church's integration within such cultures and communities. Therefore tainting any hope of changing hearts and minds and chipping away at the walls of misogyny. He chose to suggest that the women of the faith bend to cultural norms without compromising the faith in any way.

For instance, focusing on 1 Corinthians 14:34–35 for a moment, Paul wrote a letter to the Corinthian church that had its moments of spiritual immaturity due to the moral deficiency of that city. One of the main goddesses of Corinth was Aphrodite. Such worship of this goddess evoked temple prostitution, so the role of women within this society was licentious. That is why Paul wrote what he wrote. He wanted the women within the church to separate themselves from the rest of society, to be more reserved and a better example.

It's a similar situation with Paul's letter to Timothy, a leader of the church in Ephesus. Paul sent him some instructions on how to care for the church in that city. Paul was addressing a specific cultural setting. So the church there wouldn't get mixed up with the twisted societal influence; which could have had a damaging effect on the new church and new believers. This explains Paul's seemingly harsh and direct words. The instruction was to be different and to separate from the cultural norms placed on women; to begin a new mindset of value and respect for all women. Although Paul said for women not to teach, we know he approves of it elsewhere because he praises the women who are leaders and deaconesses of the church.

These questionable passages are not universal and timeless declarations. They are suggestions that were meant for a particular people group, for a certain point in time. Paul was simply giving instructions to integrate into stubborn cultural societies, so that the new message could be openly heard and be more effective. If women were seen to preach, teach and have equality with men, the hostile culture would have rejected any such teachings, and they would not have taken the women seriously. Paul was being sensitive to the cultural environment at the time without necessarily agreeing with it. It would be like if you went to a foreign land with deep cultural beliefs that have been the social norm for hundreds of years. Going to the public square, stepping up on your soapbox, and shouting, 'Hey, you guys have got it all wrong, you should be living another way'. You would be chased out of that land in seconds, and you may even have your life threatened. So Paul stayed sensitive to the deeply held social constructs for the sake of women, in the hope that minds and hearts would be changed from within, over time, without any external force.

Another questionable scripture that is constantly brought up is Ephesians 5:22, '*Wives submit to your husbands*'. There's a lot more to this verse and subsequent verses than meets the eye. Yet many seem to cut out this small section of scripture and use it to back up their assertion that Christianity and the Bible oppresses women. This is an intellectually dishonest claim. This passage written to the Ephesian Church is in relation to the household structure. Structures exist in many areas of life, such as places of employment, educational institutions, and governments. Without such structures in life, there would be disorder and chaos, the household is no different. Note, this passage does not say, 'women submit to men,' it is within a family/domestic situation, husbands and wives. The word 'submit' or 'submission' is not a popular word in this day and age, it seems to have a negative meaning to it. But from a biblical perspective, it's said in a positive light and by no means places women in an inferior status or role. The New Testament biblical texts were written mostly in the Greek language and many words written in the Greek language lose their true meaning when translated to English. The Greek word for submission, in this text, means to, '*Willingly place oneself under the authority of another*'. It's not about coercion by the other person. I believe that the suggestion for women to willingly submit to their husbands is because they're more capable of doing so. If we're being honest, most men can be stubborn, pride-filed and pig-headed. Women on the other hand are naturally more temperate, more understanding, and more willing to submit, something that a man, in his nature, would find difficult to do.

It's not all one-way traffic. If you read on, there are statements like '*Husbands, love your wives just as Christ loved the church and gave himself up for her'* (v. 25). *'Husbands ought to love their wives as their own bodies, he who loves his wife loves himself'* (v. 28). *'A man will leave his father and mother and be united to his wife'* (v. 31). In these passages the husband is to honour, love and respect his wife, even give up his life for her if it's called for. Such is the responsibility of the man in the family unit, a lot more is demanded from him. Again these verses aren't strict declarations but rather sound instructions to have a peaceful and loving household. Mutual respect and honour are biblically foundational to a home and family unit, especially between husband and wife.

The same instructions for wives to submit, and husbands to respect and honour their wives, are found in Colossians (chapter 3, vv.18–19). Colossae was a Roman province. These instructions were given to the first-century household which was a very patriarchal and authoritarian institution. In Roman culture, the husband held the power of life and death over his wife and children. So these biblical instructions greatly increase the rights of women within the household, and it's the wife's choice if she wants to willingly allow her husband to take the lead of the household. These scriptural instances are under the heading, *Instructions for Christian Households*. Note the key word there, *instructions*, it's not a rule or law.

I chose these examples to explain the meanings behind such passages. There are some other remarks about women that come across as unsavoury and derogatory, but these texts should not be taken at face value. Rather, an understanding of the context must be applied. But the number of passages that affirm women and their role within the church and society, far outweigh the questionable ones. The subsequent writings and teachings of Jesus' followers do not contradict what Jesus taught, in fact, they support how he respected and treated women. It's been said that Christianity in the first few centuries, was known as the *women's religion*, because it valued and esteemed women as equals, more so than any other faith or people group at the time. Jesus' teachings are as relevant back then as they are today. Unfortunately, there are still many sections of society, including some church denominations, that don't fully recognise the worth and value of women, especially in certain regions of the world.

Some might argue, why didn't Jesus choose at least one woman within his inner circle of 12 disciples? It's not known for certain. But I would say that to include a woman, or women, within his inner circle of disciples would have been too polarising for the male-dominated society to accept. If he did have women as his closest disciples, perhaps many would not have taken him seriously, including his own disciples. The fact he allowed women to be followers, supporters, and openly taught them, was controversial enough and drew the ire of many, especially the religious elite. So consideration must be applied when reading the teachings of Jesus and his followers throughout the New Testament texts. Jesus and his followers encountered hostile societies with well-established cultural prejudices and deeply ingrained biases toward women. Although he didn't break down the patriarchal system in one big swoop, he and his followers implemented some revolutionary changes at the time. The scriptural evidence is overwhelming, that Jesus was a true champion for women's rights and equality. Not just how he treated and valued women, but the legacy he left for his followers to follow.

Slavery

I've heard it said many times that the Bible approves of slavery. This claim is uneducated, absolutely false, and contradicts Jesus' teachings. In this chapter, we'll look specifically into the scriptural references about slavery and clear up the general misconceptions about the texts. There are a few passages about slavery throughout the Bible that, at face value, seem to approve of slavery. But these texts must be read in context and the time of these writings must be taken into account. Jesus' teachings infer that every human being has intrinsic value. Therefore to debase another human being is absolutely evil.

In Jesus' time, a slave owner had the right to execute a slave for any wrongdoing. Jesus turned it around to execute slavery. His followers carried on his teachings as I will point out in this chapter. First of all, let's take a look at slavery 2000 years ago in the Roman Empire. More than half the population within the Roman Empire were slaves. Slavery then was not based on ethnicity or the colour of a person's skin, as we know racism from the nineteenth and twentieth centuries. Slaves were mostly non-citizens of the ruling Empire and it was part of the social and economic structure. The slave industry was the pillar of the Roman workforce. Being a slave at that time, in most cases, meant better living conditions than those who weren't slaves. Lawyers, Teachers and Doctors were considered slaves. Many slaves were better placed economically and had better living conditions than people that weren't slaves. So slavery had a different meaning within the Roman Empire compared to how we know slavery today. However, there were terrible instances of slave abuse, such as; torture, beatings and even death if a slave stepped out of line. It's this type of mistreatment of slaves that Jesus and his followers addressed without completely condemning slavery.

It is unfair to assert, that Jesus and his followers approve of slavery just because there are no specific texts where they condemn slavery. Granted, the scriptures don't straight-up condemn slavery but neither do they commend slavery. Rather, the teaching and advice given within these texts were given for the reality of the times. You have to understand that Jesus and his followers were living in an incredibly stubborn society with a well-established mindset of owning slaves. To come out and declare the end of slavery, a practice that has been in place for hundreds of years, simply wouldn't fly. It would get shot down immediately and they themselves would be imprisoned, if not murdered for insurrection against the government, then what use would they be?

Instead, slavery had to be gradually broken down from within. Jesus and his followers could have approached the issue from the outside with force and coercion but that would initiate conflict, which was not Jesus' way. For a real and lasting change, it had to come from the heart and not be forced. That's the way they attacked slavery. As we will see from the following texts, these passages are directed at slaves and their owners. Jesus didn't specifically address the topic of slavery, but there is more than enough evidence to suggest Jesus' disapproval of slave abuse. His concern, care and treatment of people regardless of their rank, social status or ethnicity indicates as such.

Jesus had three years to minister to the masses and more specifically to his disciples who were to carry on his teachings. Jesus saw attitudes in the disciples that reflected the distorted societal norms. He knew he had to change their hearts first and foremost. So his focus was on his immediate followers and that's probably why we don't read much about his teachings on slavery to the larger crowds. However, there is no misunderstanding about Jesus' affirmation of the value and dignity of human beings, regardless of their background. Most of the texts about slavery are in the remainder of the New Testament books following the Gospels.

There was an instance where the disciples were arguing amongst themselves, about who is the greatest among them. Jesus told them, '*Anyone who wants to be first must be the very last, and the servant of all*' (Mark 9:35). Why do people have slaves? Because they think they are greater and more powerful than others, Jesus saw this in their argument. Their mentality was still stuck in a 'mightier than thou' attitude and he made sure he drilled the message home that no one is greater than another. Jesus also put it another way to his disciples, '*Those who exalt themselves will be humbled, and those who humble themselves will be exalted*' (Matthew 23:12). The biggest example of humility and service Jesus showed his disciples was when he washed their feet (John 13:1–17). This would have shocked them. That their teacher and Lord who they greatly revere and respect serve them, the students. The disciple Peter, who had previously declared

Jesus as the Son of God, refused at first in allowing Jesus to wash his feet (v. 8). He knew in that culture, that the job of foot washing was reserved for a lowly servant. The disciples held the view that they were subservient to Jesus. They believed that Jesus was who he said he was, the Son of God. So when Jesus said things like, '*I no longer call you servants...I call you friends...*' (John 15:15). '*I did not come to be served but to serve*' (Matthew 20:28); this would have had a profound impact on their deeply held societal beliefs. By washing their feet, Jesus gave a fine example of serving each other in humility (John 13:13–15), not lording it over another. If we're serving each other in love and humility, this breaks down the institution of slavery. The disciples eventually understood the teachings of Jesus. So how did they put Jesus' teachings into action? Let's have a look at some of the texts on slavery.

The New Testament book of Philemon is mostly about slavery, and how followers of Jesus are to treat slaves. More specifically the story is about a runaway slave. Paul writes a letter to a member of the church, Philemon, to take back his runaway slave, Onesimus, who had been with Paul and had become a believer. A runaway slave could be tortured and put to death as were the owner's rights. So why would Paul suggest Philemon take back Onesimus? Shouldn't he have told Onesimus to get away while he can? Philemon was a member of the church and Paul, a church superior. Paul could have told Philemon to give Onesimus his freedom. Paul really took on Jesus' teaching by not having a 'morally superior' type of attitude. Paul was held in high regard within the church and he could have coerced Philemon to let Onesimus go. Rather, in verse 8 he said, '*Although in Christ I could be*

46

bold and order you to do what you ought to do', he continues in verse 9, *'yet I prefer to appeal to you on the basis of love'*. Paul's insistence that Onesimus be sent back to Philemon is because it was the right thing to do. If he had kept him, it would have been illegal according to the laws of the time. His desire was for the two to be reconciled, something that could not happen if Onesimus did not return. Here's the thing about how Paul handled the situation. He pleads for Onesimus and requests that Philemon take Onesimus back, *'No longer as a slave, but better than a slave, as a dear brother'* (v. 16). This is an extraordinary request, even more so than asking Philemon to set him free. To accept a slave, a runaway slave at that, as a brother, his equal, is unheard of. That would have been very difficult for any slave owner to do. That's why Paul appeals on the basis of love. So here we see Paul, not advocating slavery but trying to change the attitude of slavery from within with love, not forcing his power or influence. If he did use coercion, Philemon would have probably let Onesimus go, but only because of guilt and shame, which wouldn't have achieved the greater 'heart' change. As I mentioned previously, real change comes from the heart and it must be a voluntary act of love. Paul even made himself a slave for Onesimus by saying, *'If he has done you any wrong or owes you anything, charge it to me'* (v. 18). A true sacrificial heart, mimicking the one he looks up to, Jesus. I think if Onesimus' life was in danger, Paul would have handled the situation differently. If the slave owner was not someone from within the church, who had vowed to kill the runaway slave, Paul would have most likely kept Onesimus safe.

So what about the questionable scriptures that seem to suggest that slaves should just suck it up? Let's go through them.

Slaves, obey your earthly masters in everything; and do it, not only when their eye is on you and to curry their favour but with sincerity of heart and reverence for the Lord. Whatever you do, work at it with all your heart, as working for the Lord, not for human masters. Colossians 3:22–23.

Slaves, obey your earthly masters with respect and fear, and with sincerity of heart, just as you would obey Christ. Obey them not only to win their favour when their eye is on you but as slaves of Christ, doing the will of God from your heart. Ephesians 6:5–6.

Teach slaves to be subject to their masters in everything, to try to please them, not to talk back to them, and not to steal from them, but to show that they can be fully trusted so that in every way they will make the teaching about God our Saviour attractive. Titus 2:9–10.

Paul's teaching about slaves obeying their earthly masters is similar to the employee and employer relationship today. Remember, at the start of the chapter, I mentioned that slavery was different 2000 years ago than how we know it today. In most instances, it's like a job, except if you stepped out of line the punishment may have been more severe than it is today.

These teachings are suggestions and not commandments to slaves on how to live in a flawed society. Paul merely pointed out the reality of the times that the slaves were living in. In the hope that the respectful and willing servitude of these slaves will themselves be a beckon of change by changing the attitudes and hearts of their earthly masters. Change is more likely to occur from love and willing service rather than a bad attitude and unwillingness. Paul's instruction wasn't just for slaves, he had some pretty severe warnings for masters, to treat their slaves with dignity and respect.

Masters, provide your slaves with what is right and fair because you know that you also have a Master in heaven. Colossians 4:1.

And masters, treat your slaves in the same way. Do not threaten them, since you know that he who is both their Master and yours is in heaven, and there is no favouritism with him. Ephesians 6:9.

Paul sums it up beautifully in Philippians 2:3, '*Value others above yourselves*'. So although the scriptures don't denounce slavery, they don't approve of the practice either. These teachings, based on dignity, respect and love; were given to slaves and slave owners in a time when slavery was a normal part of society. At that time, slavery could not have been abolished in one swoop. It had to be done bit by bit, spearheaded by Jesus' command to, '*love one another*' (John 13:34). The goal was to change hearts and mindsets. To change the relationship between owner and slave, into brothers and sisters, was quite revolutionary for that time. To lead a forceful revolt against the system would have caused great uproar and violence and cause many casualties. This approach would not have achieved much. I'm sure the ruling tyrannical Roman government would have crushed any type of opposition in a few short moments.

It is distressing that slavery, the type of slavery that subtracts the value and dignity of human life, exists today more so than at any other time in history. Due to the clandestine nature of slavery, it's difficult to ascertain the numbers. It's estimated that approximately 50 million people are caught up in the institution of human trafficking and slavery in some form. Most of which are women and children. Followers of Jesus today lead the charge against human trafficking in advocacy, prevention, rescue and rehabilitation.

Racism

There are white supremacy groups that claim to be 'Christian'. They cherry-pick certain Bible quotes (specifically from the Old Testament) to justify their racism. They are completely taking these texts out of context. As a side note, it's quite ironic that these groups have racist attitudes toward Jewish people, yet they claim to follow and worship Jesus, who is a Jew. This goes to show how skewed their views really are.

Two thousand years ago, there was such intense hatred and dislike for different cultures and races. Probably more so than at any other time in history. This especially existed between the Jews and, in particular, the Samaritans. The Romans disliked the Jews, the Jews disliked the Romans, the Jews disliked anyone that wasn't a Jew and the list goes on and on. Jesus again had to deal with stubborn hard-hearted ingrained cultural biases where it was expected that interaction was with your own kind only. So what does Jesus say about racism and how did he approach the issue?

Jesus spoke and spent time with people from many different backgrounds, races and beliefs. At that time, people wouldn't have associated with another person that was not of their own kind. Before I go on, I want to define a word that may not be known to all, the word, *Gentile*, means someone who is not Jewish. Jesus' lineage included Jews and Gentiles, the fact that his family ancestry doesn't pertain to one race says a lot. There are some controversial New Testament texts that some might say promotes racism. Let's delve into these texts more closely.

A Canaanite woman, a Gentile, approached Jesus pleading that he would heal her daughter (Matthew 15:21–28). At first, Jesus didn't answer her, most likely to see how the disciples would respond. They told him to, '*send her away*' (v. 23). Then Jesus answered the woman, '*I was sent only to the lost sheep of Israel*' (v. 24), he means the Jewish people. The woman pleaded further and Jesus said, '*It is not right to take the children's bread and toss it to the dogs*' (v. 26). Why would Jesus say such things? His remarks seem racist. Firstly, the term 'dogs' was not Jesus' own reference for non-Jews. It was a common slur used by the Jewish people for anyone that wasn't a Jew. It was a cruel term referencing rough, wild dogs. But when Jesus used the term, he took the harshness out of it, rather the term he used meant 'little dogs' or pet dogs around the dinner table. This is another instance where the original meaning gets lost in the English translation. Some historians suggest he may have said it with sarcasm. The fact that the woman persisted suggests she understood the metaphor and that Jesus spoke with gentleness. If he was aggressive, the woman would have most likely gone away. Also, note that Jesus didn't send her away as the disciples requested, he respected this woman's faith. Because of her, *great faith* (v. 28), and despite her racial, and gender persuasion, Jesus granted her request and her daughter was healed. No doubt to the surprise of the disciples. In this whole episode, Jesus was teaching his disciples an important lesson. The story starts off by saying Jesus withdrew to, *Tyre and Sidon*, these were Gentile territories. After the interaction with the woman, Jesus left there and went along, *the Sea of Galilee* (v. 29), a Jewish territory. It's like he went there for the sole purpose of encountering the Canaanite woman and teaching his disciples about acceptance, regardless of race.

Another controversial passage is in the book of Matthew, chapter 10, verses 5–6. Jesus said to his disciples as he sent them out to heal and preach the message, *'Do not go among the Gentiles or enter any town of the Samaritans. Go rather to the lost sheep of Israel'*. Why would Jesus say this if he accepted people regardless of race? This is because it was the disciple's first mission to heal and preach. They were still oblivious to Jesus' message of, *acceptance regardless of race*, and have not yet fully shaken off their deeply held prejudices. The motive behind Jesus' seemingly racial remarks had to do with the disciples and had nothing to do with racism. As we saw in the previous example of the Canaanite woman (which happened after the disciples were sent out), the disciples still had racist views. Jesus knew this and so he asked them to focus on the Jewish people first so as not to be distracted from the core purpose. I guess this was an exercise for them to get some practice before they reached out to everyone from different races and backgrounds after Jesus' resurrection. If Jesus had requested they preach to the Gentiles in their first attempt, it would have been incredibly hard for them. No doubt it would have been done with disdain and insincerity. Which would have caused more harm than good. So, for their first mission Jesus got them to focus on the Jewish race, their own kind, for their sake but also for the sake of the Gentiles.

When Jesus wanted to teach the Gentiles, he did it himself. He knew the disciples were not ready for that yet. The disciples followed but it was Jesus that taught and interacted, like when Jesus attempted to go through Samaria (Luke 9:51–56) and when he went to the Gentile territory of Gerasenes (Mark 5:1).

It should be noted that Jesus did not reject anyone regardless of their faith, culture or race. Jesus makes it clear that those of non-Jewish backgrounds were always part of the plan to be saved. He said in John 10:16, '*I have other sheep that are not of this sheep pen. I must bring them also*', referring to the non-Jewish people. Another instance where Jesus assists a Gentile is when he grants the request of a Centurion (Roman Official) to heal his beloved servant (Luke 7:1–10). Again showing his followers that Jesus doesn't judge by race or cultural difference. In one of Jesus' most controversial moments, he zealously clears the temple because it was turned into a marketplace (John 2:13–16). He made a whip and turned over the tables, scattered the coins and drove out the people and the animals being sold. I'd like to add that Jesus didn't harm anyone in this episode or ever, for that matter. You might be thinking what does, 'Jesus clearing the temple', have to do with racism? The moneychangers and merchants were occupying the temple areas of the Gentiles, which therefore impeded their worship. According to Mark's account, Jesus states, '...*My house will be called a house of prayer for **all nations**'*, (emphasis mine), (Mark 11:17). This shows how much God desired everyone to come to him, regardless of race.

Jesus spoke about 'love for others' on many occasions. Never once did he specify whom we are to love. Instead, we are to love and respect everyone, regardless of race and cultural differences.

Moving on from the questionable scriptures to a well-known parable called, *the Good Samaritan* (Luke 10:25–37). It's about helping someone who is in need, but there are subtle points in this story that are mostly overlooked. It's not just a story about helping people in need, it's an illuminating story about racism. Before I delve into the underlying meaning of this parable, I want to give you a bit of background about the relationship between the Jews and Samaritans. To say they hated each other would be putting it nicely. Their dislike for each other was fierce and well-established. We're talking hundreds of years of hatred simply because of race and religious ethnicity. The Samaritans were a type of half-breed of the Jewish people. They set up different places of worship and throughout history, they attacked each other's Temples. They called each other names and Jews avoided going through Samaria even if it meant going the longer route. There is a lot more I can write about their hostilities toward each other but I think you get the picture. The disciples themselves showed intense hatred toward the Samaritans. Wanting to call down fire from heaven to destroy them when the Samaritans didn't welcome Jesus while on his way to Jerusalem. But Jesus rebuked them (Luke 9:51–56). So now that you know the hostility they had toward each other, this story will pack more punch.

The story of the Good Samaritan begins with an expert of the law, a Jewish religious leader asking Jesus what it takes to get to heaven. Jesus asks him what he thinks. The expert of the law responds with, among other things, '*Love your neighbour as yourself*'. Jesus affirms his response. The expert of the law wanted to justify himself and so he asked, '*Who is my neighbour?*' (Luke 10:29). He wanted to set his barriers and parameters of generosity, who to help and who he can ignore. The story of the Good Samaritan shows that we are to love all people, even those we may dislike; not just because of race, religion or cultural difference but for any other reason. In the story, a man was attacked by robbers. His clothes stripped off and left half dead (v. 30), in other words, the man was unconscious. Anyone that passed the injured man was not able to determine his ethnicity. In those days, you were able to discern a person's background by their attire, but he was stripped of his clothes. He was unconscious, not able to speak. His accent and language could not be ascertained. So here we have an unidentifiable man in need of help. Lying on the floor in an incredibly racially tense society where help was given to your own kind only. Three men pass the injured man on the road. Two of them were Jewish, and when they saw the injured man, they walked by. The third man that walked by was a Samaritan. He helped the injured man. Jesus then asks which of the men that passed by, acted as a neighbour to the injured man (v. 36)? The expert of the law responds, '*The one who had mercy on him*' (v. 37). He couldn't even bring himself to say, *the Samaritan*. That's how much they despised them. Jesus wanted to show his acceptance of other races. He intentionally portrayed the Samaritan as the good guy in this story, better than the two religious Jews that walked by (vv. 31–32). The words 'good' and 'Samaritan' were definitely not used in the same sentence at that time by the Jewish people.

Jesus was teaching that we shouldn't just help someone because they believe like you, are from the same culture as you, or are of the same nationality as you. The focus should not be on the external. You should help others simply because they are human beings that are valued by God. The man robbed, left naked and unconscious on the road, was a human being. His ethnicity and any other differences are irrelevant. The message of this parable was to challenge the deeply held prejudices of the time. It was recorded so that many generations throughout time would understand that our neighbour is not just those of our kind, our religion, or our race; our neighbour is the whole of mankind, for we are all part of one humanity.

The story about the woman at the well (John 4:1–26), where Jesus conversed with a Samaritan woman, shows how Jesus broke down the walls of racism. The Jewish custom taught not to eat even a mouthful of anything that belongs to a Samaritan. To do so would be a vile act and would make you unclean. So when Jesus asked for a drink of water from this woman's own jar (v. 7), he smashed the hostile racial boundary created by hatred and division. The woman was shocked by his asking (v. 9). She knew of the racial boundary lines. But Jesus continued to talk with her and tell her some amazing truths and insights that he had yet to tell people of his own race.

After Jesus' resurrection, we see that the disciples understood and practised what he taught. In the book of Acts, we read that the disciples go to Samaria, preaching in many Samaritan Villages (Acts 8:25). However in some instances, Peter wrestled with the deeply ingrained social constructs he grew up with. Called, *the Rock*, by Jesus, he had a special part to play in the continuance of the gospel message after Jesus' ministry on earth. As an adherent to the Jewish faith there were some deeply held beliefs Peter needed to shake off which included, a *them & us* mentality; 'us' being those pertaining to the Jewish race, and 'them' being everyone else who wasn't Jewish. A Roman named Cornelius had summoned Peter to his house (Acts 10:22–35). Peter made it clear to all there what the Jewish cultural law states, '*You are well aware that it is against our law for a Jew to associate with or visit a Gentile. But God has shown me that I should not call anyone impure or unclean*' (v. 28). Later in that passage Peter states, '*I now realise how true it is that God does not show favouritism*' (v. 34). This was also echoed by Paul in Romans 2:11.

In Romans 16:1–16, Paul lists the names of those that have served in the church, there is a great diversity of people. The names listed suggest Jews, Geeks and Romans. Names of slaves and names associated with great wealth were also mentioned. So regardless of the person's race, rank or ethnicity, all were accepted within the Church. There are several references in scripture that break down the differences we use to divide.

There is no difference between Jew and Gentile—the same Lord is Lord of all and richly blesses all who call on him. Romans 10:12.

For we were all baptised by one Spirit so as to form one body—whether Jews or Gentiles, slave or free—and we were all given the one Spirit to drink. 1 Corinthians 12:13.

Here there is no Gentile or Jew, circumcised or uncircumcised, barbarian, Scythian, slave or free, but Christ is all and is in all. Colossians 3:11.

Race, language, social standing, the colour of skin, ability, and all the vices we use to discriminate were tenaciously taught against by Jesus and his followers. Jesus led the way to destroy the racial barriers of hatred and disunity in a culturally hostile society. The disciples showed that they understood Jesus' stance about racism, continuing to preach the message and interact with Gentiles as we can see throughout the New Testament. In fact, James states it quite clearly, '*My brothers and sisters, believers in our glorious Lord Jesus Christ must not show favouritism*' (James 2:1).

Politics

In this politically charged world we live in, many wonder what side of politics is Jesus on. Does Jesus stand with those on the left or does he stand with those on the right? Would he be wearing red or blue? Would he side with Liberals or Conservatives? The chasm between left and right seems to be getting wider as time goes on. Debates between politicians, friends, families and strangers are becoming heatedly passionate, with some disagreements turning into a hotbed of violence. Protests and new movements are increasing, all adding to the reality that we're moving further away from each other. The pressure to take sides is being thrust upon us. Making it harder to meet in the middle and to respect each other's views and differences of opinion. Some followers of Jesus seem to think that whatever political persuasion they adhere to is the one that Jesus definitely supports.

The political landscape in Jesus' time was as emotionally charged as it is today. There is strong evidence within the Gospels that suggests where Jesus stands in the political arena and we'll look at that in this chapter.

Government

Jesus laid the platform for his followers to be model citizens within every society. To be respectful and not trouble-makers. First of all, let's look at what Jesus said and how he lived under the government. Jesus lived a relatively quiet life under a ruling tyrannical Roman government. Any hype and hysteria about Jesus were instigated by other people and not himself. Not once did he say or do anything to suggest an overthrow or revolt against the government in power. In fact, he suggested the people respect the ruling authorities. There's an instance where the religious leaders asked Jesus if it was right to obey the government (Matthew 22:17–21). They specifically asked if it is right to pay taxes to Caesar (v. 17). Jesus replied, '*Show me the coin used for paying the tax*', then asked, '*Whose image and inscription is on the coin?*' (v. 20). '*Caesar's*', they replied. Then Jesus said to them, '*Give back to Caesar what is Caesar's, and to God what is God's*' (v. 21). In effect, Jesus is suggesting to the crowd to pay the government what is owed, after all the government provides services and looks after the citizens. The truth is, societies need to be governed otherwise there would be chaos. Jesus is saying that having a government to look after the country and its people is a good thing. But he is not affirming the terrible acts some governments commit. The second part of Jesus' remark where he said, '*give to God what is God's*'. This was a message to the religious leaders and the people who were obsessed with overthrowing the current rulers and forming their own government. He was saying to get over the obsession to bring down the current government and focus rather on changing their own hearts to foster a better society. A forceful change to a more favourable government would only bring up a new set of governing issues. It shows that Jesus' agenda was not at all political. Rather it was all about overthrowing the condition of the human heart, not earthly ruling authorities or governments. You don't get lasting and positive change by changing the government. True and lasting change comes from the heart of each individual. The history of rulers, as well as modern-day governments, show us that no matter what type of government is in control, they all have their cringe-worthy moments.

Jesus didn't attempt to gain power nor did he instruct his followers to do so. In fact, when the people tried to make him king, he fled (John 6:15). Instead, Jesus taught us to live in humility and to serve one another. I hear a lot of people bring up the Christian Crusades. They ask how that reconciles with Jesus' teachings. Well, it doesn't. If you get to know Jesus, you will find that he is the most peaceful and loving man that has ever walked the earth. The Crusaders were retaliating in relation to the Arab Conquests in the seventh century. They fought back to repossess land that was stolen and liberate the Christians living under tyranny. Some might say it was noble that they saved the oppressed, however, in many instances they went too far in their violent crusade. They were really fighting for themselves, to gain control and power. The Christian Crusaders got it wrong. Never once did Jesus teach us to fight back. In fact, when he was arrested (Matthew 26:47–54), one of his disciples reached for his sword and cut off the high priest's servant's ear. Jesus rebuked the disciple and commanded him to put the sword away. There's no relation to the ill-actions of the Crusaders, and other groups of so-called Christians throughout history and even today, to Jesus and his teachings.

What about the disciples of Jesus, what did they have to say about the government? What they wrote can be construed as questionable but again, these texts must be read in context. Let's take a look at some of these texts.

Submit yourselves for the Lord's sake to every human authority: whether to the emperor, as the supreme authority, or to governors, who are sent by him to punish those who do wrong and to commend those who do right. 1 Peter 2:13–14.

Remind the people to be subject to rulers and authorities, to be obedient, to be ready to do whatever is good. Titus 3:1.

These texts, and others like them, no doubt will raise a few eyebrows. Like many other texts that need to be read in context, these are instructions, not commands. Written for the early church if they wanted to live a peaceful life under the current ruling government. At that time, if anyone stepped out of line, the punishment was severe, hence the warnings to obey. If today I damaged another person's property or committed tax fraud, I would be punished by the authorities with a fine or short incarceration. However, under the ruling Roman government, the punishment could be death for someone who wasn't a Roman citizen. Is there a time when we should question, disobey or stand up to the government? Absolutely yes! When governments commit acts of injustice and oppression that devalue the sanctity of human life. That's when we need to be a voice and protect those that are being violated. The followers of Jesus showed that even though they obeyed and respected authority. They spoke out when it contradicted a higher authority, '*We must obey God rather than human beings*' (Acts 5:29). Most of Jesus' followers were executed by the Roman authorities because of their convictions. They could have recanted to save their lives but they didn't, holding to the higher truth. Thankfully, in this day and age, we won't be put to death for disagreeing and speaking out against the government, well not in most of the western world anyway.

Left or Right?

I often wondered if Jesus walked the earth today, which side of politics he would be on. I think it's a fairly important question in the current political environment, especially for those who call themselves followers of Jesus. Clarity is needed as we've descended to an 'us' and 'them' mentality, with factions and sides declaring that Jesus stands with them. The answer is found in the gospels. More specifically, with two of the disciples he chose. I believe Jesus gave the world this illustration so we don't use politics as a divisive weapon to divide.

It's fair to say that Jesus chose a rag-tag bunch of guys to be his close followers. When you read the Gospels, you get to know more about what some of the disciples were like. Peter was profane and hot-tempered (Matthew 26:74; John 18:10); James and John were self-centred and vengeful (Mark 10:35–37; Luke 9:54); Thomas was a doubter (John 20:25) and Judas Iscariot was a betrayer and a thief (Matthew 26:25; John 12:6). It's the disciples Matthew and Simon that sheds light on where Jesus stands on the political scale. Matthew (also known as Levi) was a Jewish tax collector. He was also a Levite. A Levite was someone from the Jewish Levitical Order. A special group of people that were set apart for a life of religious devotion. Matthew turned his back on his Jewish religious lineage to work with the oppressive Roman government to collect taxes from his own people. This meant that he earned his living charging a little extra on top of the official Roman tax to line his own pockets. To say that his own people hated him would be an understatement. They would have loathed him and even excommunicated him from the Jewish religious life. He was considered one of the worst sinners under religious law. In terms of political persuasions, Matthew would have been deemed as someone on the political extremist right.

The other disciple Jesus chose in his inner circle was Simon the Zealot. The *Zealot,* reference was someone that held strong extremist religious and political views and would have been staunchly against the ruling Roman occupation. The Zealot sect would have been relentless in their pursuit of establishing their ideals. It is debated if being a Zealot was someone that was part of a fierce and somewhat violent political group that was opposed to anything 'Roman'; or if the term Zealot was given to someone that was extremely fanatical about their Jewish heritage and religion. Either way, there would have been a strong dislike for the Roman occupation and for anyone who associated themselves with the government, like Mathew the tax collector. In terms of political persuasions, Simon would have been deemed as someone on the political extremist left.

The scriptures don't give an indication of how the disciples got along with each other apart from a few small arguments. It would have been interesting to see how Matthew and Simon got along with each other if they even did speak to each other at all. So why did Jesus choose two disciples that held distinctly opposing views to each other? You couldn't have chosen two people so far apart from each other in regards to political views than Matthew and Simon. I believe Jesus chose these two disciples as an example for us today. Jesus did not create or take sides; nor did he form exclusive political groups. Instead, he removed the barriers of division and separation to include everyone from all walks of political life. Jesus' example should inspire us to find common ground, despite political views so that we can all work together for the greater good of humanity. Jesus understands the reality of the human heart. We're not going to agree with each other all the time. We will encounter some that have completely opposite, and even more extreme views than our own. But that shouldn't stop us from loving and respecting each other and working together to create a better society for all people. Jesus showed us that he didn't just mingle and hang out with those that believed exactly like he did, he was all-inclusive. So I think it's fair to say that Jesus doesn't stand on one side of the political spectrum, but if you must label him, I guess you can say he is smack-bang in the centre.

It's a great illustration for all of us regardless of what side we stand on; what political or religious belief, or none, you adhere to. Let's all meet together in the centre and work together. That's not to say we won't have disagreements on certain issues, of course, we will. We're individuals with strong and deeply held beliefs and convictions. But as Jesus shows us, we can still respect each other and we can still love each other by not focusing on what divides us. Instead focusing on what unites us; that we're all part of humanity and we can still work together for the greater cause.

Ethics and Morality

Who can we trust to set the moral standard? What or who defines right and wrong? What a government or culture mandates as legal or illegal doesn't mean it's moral or ethical. Let's be honest, human beings are flawed so who is worthy to create humanity's moral code? In order for morality to be objective, there must be a mind that exists separate from the human mind. Otherwise, ethics and morality, right or wrong, are relative and based on an individual, cultural or government preference. What's right for one person, culture or nation; might be wrong for another person, culture or nation, and so there must be a basis for objective morality that transcends the human mind. Otherwise, we are stuck in moral relativism, making absolute morality, obsolete. New Testament biblical texts claim that Jesus was perfect, inferring he didn't sin (1 Peter 2:22; 2 Corinthians 5:21; Hebrews 4:15; 1 John 3:5). Jesus didn't write these things about himself, rather the eye witnesses wrote about his sinless life. In one instance, Jesus challenged the crowd by saying, '*Can any of you prove me guilty of sin*' (John 8:46); no one could challenge him on that. If his claims of sinlessness are true, then he would be an appropriate source of objective morality. When you read and study the life and teachings of Jesus, you will discover that he lays the platform for ethics and morality. The foundations being, character, relationships and principles, with the founding principle being love.

There were many instances where Jesus went against the flow of what was culturally and civically acceptable. It was morally acceptable to stone the woman caught in the act of adultery, but Jesus stepped in to save her life (John 8:3–11). It was socially acceptable not to associate with people of ill-repute yet Jesus loved and spent time with such people, even allowing them into his inner circle. It was taboo for teachers to teach and speak to women, yet he did just that. At that time, the concept of treating all humans equal did not exist. In all cultures, men had more value and worth than women and children. In certain cultures and thoughts of philosophy, newborns would be discarded based on their gender (mostly girls) or disability—unfortunately, infanticide still occurs in certain cultures today. When Jesus came on to the scene, he smashed apart the unethical practice of devaluing human life. He treated women equally and raised their status in society. He embraced children and allowed them to come to him. He spent time with the vulnerable and disabled and healed them. Jesus shows that all human life has innate worth and value. To degrade and mistreat any human life is immoral.

Jesus taught some of the greatest ethical teachings ever recorded in the book of Matthew, chapters five to seven, also referred to as the Sermon on the Mount. In these three chapters, we read how Jesus turns worldly constructs upside down and delves deeper into the heart of ethics and morality. His teachings on ethics and morality are as relevant today as they were 2000 years ago. Especially in this age where values are being overtaken by, *what feels good.*

Starting off with the Beatitudes (Matthew 5:1–11). In Jesus' time, even in our world today, the mighty, powerful and the rich are adored and even regarded as premier human beings by many because of their status. This so-called 'high-class' form of humanity is a breeding ground for arrogance, some using their privilege as they please. Jesus took the opposite view and praised the humble in spirit, and the meek. As a side note, meekness doesn't mean weakness; rather, it's strength under control. If we drill down to many of the world's issues, pride and arrogance would be at the centre. This isn't just an issue of the rich, famous and powerful, but society in general. How often do we perpetuate conflicts on a communal or family level? If everyone exercised humility, gentleness and respect, our world, societies and homes will be better places to live. Here Jesus is showing us the moral principle of valuing others above yourself (Philippians 2:3).

Jesus goes on to say that murder is not just about taking the life of another but is the act of being angry at someone (Matthew 5:21–26). Anger in this passage means to be enraged; an intense feeling of displeasure and hostility. In other words, hatred. Jesus instructs us to do everything in our power to reconcile with others as quickly as possible. Jesus knew if the issue of a hateful heart is allowed to fester, it could lead to stubbornness of the heart, even to the point of taking another life. Here Jesus is laying the ethical platform of love and forgiveness.

Adultery is not just about the act itself but about looking at another with lust (Matthew 5:27–30). This isn't just targeted toward married people, but everyone. All eventual acts of adultery begin with that first lustful look. This verse isn't talking about admiring someone's beauty. But rather a prolonged stare, igniting wayward thoughts that initiate a corrupt craving for another. Jesus uses hyperbole to suggest the seriousness of this issue. If we're being honest, this is mostly a male issue. I've heard it said many times, there's no harm in looking. Maybe not at first, but there's no telling what will develop from that initial lustful stare. We are fickle beings that give way to strong feelings of desire. Sadly, many men have acted on their evil lustful desires and have forced themselves on women, and violating them. Even taking their lives to hide their evil acts. Jesus is saying that we're more than our outward appearance, we have a heart and a soul— which is the real identity of every person. To reduce the value of someone by their appearance is to make them objects, devaluing them as human beings. This passage also acts as a safeguard for women. To protect them from a patriarchal society, where in some countries today women's rights are non-existent.

His teachings about divorce provide protection for women at a time when husbands could have discarded their wives for menial reasons, therefore leaving them destitute (Matthew 5:31–32). Here Jesus is teaching that everyone is valuable and has intrinsic worth in the eyes of God. Regardless of how society, culture or others deem their value and worth.

Jesus taught us not to seek revenge upon anyone or retaliate over small matters. Many of us tend to respond harshly when we've been wronged or told something that we find offence with. Jesus teaches to turn the other cheek (Matthew 5:38–42), meaning, don't retaliate. This is in relation to a personal insult or wrongdoing. Our natural inclination is to do or say something as a type of 'payback'. This will continue the cycle of vengeance and hatred. At a time when paying back your enemy was an acceptable and expected practice, Jesus turned the tables. He taught us to love our enemies and to pray for them and even to do good toward them (Matthew 5:43–48). Let the matter end with you and respond with love and kindness. However, this doesn't relate to physical abuse. If an aggressor is physically harming you or others, certainly don't turn the other cheek and do nothing. If possible, step up to protect yourself and others, even if it means harming the aggressor, and get help if necessary. Jesus wants us to be guided by peace. Peace within and peace with others. When we live by the guiding ethical principle of peace, our lives are simply better, and we're healthier and happier. Paul wrote, *'If it is possible, as far as it depends on you, live at peace with everyone'* (Romans 12:18). You'll notice that Paul said, *'If it is possible, as far as it depends on you...'* The reality is, not everyone will want to reconcile with you or make things right with you, in which case, leave them be. But if possible, continue to do good toward them, radiating kindness.

At the beginning of chapter six, Jesus teaches about giving. Not how much to give but how to give. It's great to give to others in need but Jesus places importance on why we give. Is it to look good in front of others or because we have a genuine concern and love for the needy? Jesus isn't suggesting that you should not give until your motives are right. If we're honest, I think we've all given out of a wrong motive at some point in our lives, and it's great to give help where it's needed regardless of the motive. But Jesus taught that it's even better to give when love is the motive. God sets the example in John 3:16, it states, *'For God so loved the world that he gave his one and only son'*. God loved, therefore he gave. You might ask, if we're giving to help others why does the motive matter? If the main motive of giving is how others will perceive you, over time pride and selfishness will build up. That pride and selfishness will permeate into other areas of your life. That's why Jesus warns us to be mindful of the motives of the heart.

Jesus doesn't want us to worry (Matthew 6:25–34). Life can be hectic and we can worry about many things. Most of our daily concerns are not necessary. When we constantly fret and worry our psychological, emotional and physical health can wane. In turn, this can cause grumpiness and stress. Not only affecting ourselves but our relationships too, adding to the already mounting concerns of the day. Jesus said to stop worrying about the lesser things of life (v. 25), and take it one day at a time (v. 34). Here Jesus is teaching us the ethical stance of taking care of yourself, not just the physical, but the mind and soul too. It's good to put others above yourself but not to the detriment of yourself, you are important too.

At the start of chapter seven, Jesus point-blank states, do not judge others. Implying that no one is perfect. This doesn't mean to cease any type of judgment. Rather, we ought to be gracious. Our judgments are not to be harsh or critical and come from a selfish 'holier-than-thou' attitude. He also said don't judge by appearance, *'Stop judging by mere appearances, but instead judge correctly'* (John 7:24). We certainly shouldn't write people off if they step out of line. You might not know the extent of the path they're on or the past they came from which could have been riddled with trauma and difficulty. To be clear, Jesus was not saying that we should overlook criminal conduct. Nor should we withhold good and constrictive advice to help others out of trouble if they're heading down a slippery slope. Nor should we excuse the acts that are harmful, to themselves or others. In essence, Jesus taught us to let him judge because he sees the heart like no one can. Our responsibility as part of humanity is to love and help others wherever and whenever we can. Moving on from the Sermon on the Mount. The story of the birth of Jesus isn't just a nice story about angels, rejoicing and peace on earth, there's a deeper meaning to it. One way to look at it is that it's a story about breaking down the walls of judgment. It also highlights tolerance, equality, and acceptance of all regardless of social standing. Let's turn to a particular part of this story about the shepherds in the field.

And there were shepherds living out in the fields nearby, keeping watch over their flocks at night. An angel of the Lord appeared to them, and the glory of the Lord shone around them, and they were terrified. But the angel said to them, 'Do not be afraid. I bring you good news that will cause great joy for all the people. Today in the town of David a Saviour has been born to you; he is the Messiah, the Lord. This will be a sign to you: You will find a baby wrapped in cloths and lying in a manger Luke 2:8–12.

Here we read that angels appear to the shepherds in the field, announcing the birth of Jesus. But why did the angels announce the birth of Jesus to shepherds? Why not announce this great news to wise scholars, the kingly rulers or the chief priests? Shepherds were considered the lowest and least of society—literally at the bottom of the social ladder. They were rejected because of their underprivileged lifestyle. They were a little rough around the edges and not likely to have been invited to banquets or as dinner guests. They were considered unclean because they hung out with animals all day so they had a particular stench about them. As a result of their perceived uncleanness, they were not allowed and even shunned, from all religious activity, which was the centre of Jewish society at that time. To add to all that, their testimony was not even valid in court, they were well and truly the lowest class of human beings at the time. Despite the judgments that society imposed on the shepherds, the announcement of Jesus' birth came to these lowly and humble shepherds. This is quite significant. Apart from the parents, they were the first eyewitnesses to Jesus' birth. In effect, the announcement of the birth of this baby, declared the *Saviour, Messiah and Lord* (Luke 2:11), is born for all. Not just for the rich and powerful, or for the most deserving and socially accepted people, but for everyone. Even those the world rejects and treats as outcasts and deems unworthy. So in the first instance of Jesus' life, as soon as he enters the world, we see the acceptance and love for all people. Creating a just, moral and ethical standard that all people are equal. This part of the story is largely overlooked but it's an incredible statement. In a world where the powerful, the wealthy, and the influential are adored and celebrated. The homeless man living in a cardboard box in a dead-end lane, rejected and overlooked by most, is as valuable as any billionaire or celebrity. He has a value higher than what society has imposed on him and he too is worthy of acceptance and love.

Leadership

History is riddled with leaders and governments that misuse their power unethically and immorally for selfish means. This is true even today. Not just political figures but wealthy, sporting and celebrity elites that are lauded with praise and adoration. Some of them even expect it because of their lofty position in the world. You wouldn't blame Jesus, who said he's the son of God, to expect such privilege and praise, but he didn't. In fact the more you read about Jesus' life, you will see that he did a lot of serving, especially to those who were lower than him on society's scale.

Being the one his followers and disciples looked up to, Jesus showed them great examples of how leaders and people of high positions should serve others. In a world where status, success and wealth were celebrated and adored, his disciples desired that worldly power and status too. They argued about who was the greatest among themselves (Mark 9:33–34). But Jesus' way of leadership was counter-cultural and inverts the worldly power structure. Jesus said, '*If anyone wants to be first, he must be the very last, and the servant of all*' (v. 35). Jesus even referred to himself, '*For even the Son on Man did not come to be served, but to serve, and to give his life as a ransom for many*' (Mark 10:45). An amazing portrayal of true leadership is when Jesus washed his disciple's feet at the Last Supper (John 13:1–17). He was showing that service and humility make a leader despite the cultural expectations of what leaders shouldn't do. In Jesus' time, washing someone's feet was a menial task, even some servants were spared from the indignity of doing this task. The main type of footwear was sandals. The streets weren't paved, so dirt was constantly flung in the air as people walked. Animals were all over the place, so when they had to go, they went right there in the street and people would have stepped in who knows what. So at the end of the day, you can imagine how dirty one's feet would have been. That's why it was considered such a lowly task. Jesus was teaching that being great is to serve. He completed a task that was culturally considered the work of a lowly slave. In other words, Jesus is implying that no task is too lowly or demeaning for his followers to perform when serving others. And this is relevant for leaders in today's world, and not just leaders but for all no matter their social standing. Another thing to note is that Jesus even washed Judas' feet. The man that betrayed him. Jesus knew he was going to do this, yet he still washed his feet. Jesus truly lived the ethical standard of humbling yourself and serving others.

Money

I've included a section about money because let's face it, money and greed are the main cause of many to compromise their ethics and morality. For some, the love of money can go too far. I've read many stories of how someone wins the lottery and their lives have been ruined. They become addicts and families break down, their stories are quite sad. Money and all things related are talked about by Jesus a fair bit. Why did Jesus talk so much about money? Because he knew the dangers of worldly wealth. How it can deceive many into a life of greed and selfishness that leads to a relentless pursuit of gaining more and more wealth at any cost, to the point of devaluing human life to get it. It is the cause of much mistreatment of others in the world today. The modern-day slave industry is driven by money; it is a billion-dollar industry. Remove the money aspect out of that industry and it will fall flat very quickly. There is a Bible verse that is often misquoted. It's mistakenly quoted, '*Money is the root of all evil*', when in fact the correct verse is, '*The love of money is the root of all evil*' (1 Timothy 6:10). The key word there being 'love'. Jesus isn't against people having money, but his teachings were about making sure money doesn't have us. There are many wealthy people that do great things with their wealth; helping the vulnerable and unfortunate, building hospitals, schools and creating a better society at large. This is what Jesus taught about, and not to hoard money for yourself. Jesus warned, '*Watch out! Be on your guard against all kinds of greed, life does not consist in an abundance of possessions*' (Luke 12:15). The Apostle Paul said that people of the faith have pierced themselves with much grief because of their love of money (1 Timothy 6:10). No one is immune to the lure of worldly wealth.

Jesus had a conversion with a rich young ruler (Matthew 19:16–22). He told the young man to sell his possessions and give to the poor (v. 21). Jesus isn't asking everyone to sell everything they own and be poor. Rather, Jesus knew that the young man's wealth had a hold of him and his heart. That's why the young man went away sad (v. 22). He couldn't part with his money because of the love he had for his wealth. It's a warning for everyone really. If you stop and think about the world today, we value possessions more than people. We spend thousands of dollars on the latest gadgets and yet human beings caught up in trafficking, mostly women and children, are being bought and sold throughout the world for a few dollars. Wealth, possessions and greed for the most part are the root of hatred, ruined relationships, wars and jealousy.

It poisons ethical and moral standards. The basis of the type of ethics and morality that Jesus taught and lived unequivocally centres on love. Not money or possessions.

Ethical practices that govern our lives should stem from the heart and be extended to all. A life of morality that clearly defines good and evil as shown by Jesus' life and teachings. To physically or psychologically harm or mistreat another human being is always evil. This doesn't mean we don't discuss topics that might offend or upset someone. Rather such discussions are to be laced with love, respect and gentleness. Jesus' teachings aren't some type of well-meaning philosophy but are meant to be a way of life for everyone to do their best to live up to. His teachings of ethics and morality should permeate throughout every aspect of society. Whether that be within the home, business, politics, or the justice system, all the way to the heart of every human being. Granted, it can be difficult to live the standard of life that Jesus lived but we can do our best every day. Then maybe, just maybe we will see a greater change in the world.

Jesus also taught it's not just about living right outwardly, although that is a good thing. Rather it's a matter of the heart. If the heart is full of goodness and love, our outward actions are then a natural by-product of that genuine love. There is a Proverb that reads, '*Above all else, guard your heart, for everything you do flows from it*' (Proverbs 4:23). There is so much truth in that proverb because all of the goodness and evil that happen in this world flows from the heart.

You might be thinking, 'How does love reconcile with ethics and morality?' Well, what are ethics and morality? It's the values and principles that dictate the way we treat others and how we distinguish between good and evil. When you narrow it down, it all points to a heart of love. If ethics and morality are created devoid of a higher standard of love, they are simply a set of rules imposed upon society and the definition is relative. But which standard of love? If we're honest, humanity's love can be tainted, and each individual has a different standard of love. The highest and perfect form of love that has ever existed is from Jesus. It's hard to argue against when you read his teachings and the way he lived his life.

In today's society, morality and ethics are driven by the desire of feelings. The modern-day mantra is, '*If it feels good, do it*'. But just because something feels good, doesn't mean it is right. If morality is guided by feelings, this makes the basis of morality and ethics unstable, drifting away from absolutes to relativism. Influential African-American educator and reformer, Booker T. Washington said it best, '*A lie doesn't become truth, wrong doesn't become right, and evil doesn't become good, just because it is accepted by a majority*'.

Love

Many non-believers today see followers of Jesus more for what they are against than what they are for. Religious hypocrisy turns many people off any ideas of religion and Jesus. The truth is though that Jesus didn't have a hypocritical bone in his body, he lived out what he preached to the letter. His main anthem was love, mercy and compassion. Which sadly, many of his followers today greatly lack. Most notably, those in religious authority can be the worst offenders.

The religious leaders of Jesus' day were void of love. They served themselves more than others. They were so full of pride that they loved the attention and being in places of prominence. So when Jesus came with a new message of love, mercy and compassion, challenging their religious system, they hated Jesus for it and tried to kill him on several occasions. He was drawing more and more people to himself every day with his new message of compassion and love, and the religious leaders didn't like the fact that their prominence was diminishing. The fact they wanted to kill him suggests they were void of love. Love at its core is to seek good for another despite their treatment towards you. Love is about giving even when you may not receive anything in return. So what did Jesus say about love?

Love for all

One of the most recognised scriptures is John 3:16, '*For God so loved the world that he gave his one and only Son, that whoever believes in him shall not perish but have eternal life*'. You will notice that it reads 'the world', not a certain group of people but everyone that has ever existed in this world. Certain Christian groups may spew out hate-filled comments like '*God hates you because you're not like me*', John 3:16 refutes that claim. God so loves everyone; he is patient with everyone; he doesn't want anyone to live apart from him (2 Peter 3:9). God desires a relationship with everyone and that's why Jesus came to earth, to show God's love for all humanity and Jesus' love doesn't discriminate. He loved regardless of the differences that many use as a tool to hate and divide, whether that was cultural, religious, ethnic, economic, social status, gender, ability and on I could go. He didn't just love from a distance. He hung out and spent time with such people when it was taboo to do so, like the people the religious leaders deemed 'sinful'. They wondered why Jesus associated with such people (Luke 5:30). Jesus loved them, not necessarily agreeing with their actions but loving the person and drawing the person to his love for them. He associated with many people that others wouldn't go anywhere near. People that were unclean, despised and hated; he also engaged with the social elite. There were no barriers with Jesus. His life is a perfect example of love for all regardless of race, gender, social standing, or religion; he did not reject anyone. Never once did he hate or harm anyone. However Jesus was harsh when it was necessary. He gave the religious leaders a piece of his mind because of their hypocrisy and lack of love (Luke 11:39–52). This is for good reason, they should have known better. Jesus knew that they were turning people off by their harsh interpretation of religion and that's why he heaped such scorn on them, but Jesus still loved them and his harsh rebuke was a warning to them.

Jesus' directive is clear, '*A new command I give you: Love one another. As I have loved you, so you must love one another. By this everyone will know that you are my disciples if you love one another*' (John 13:34–35). The Greek translation of the word, *love,* in this passage, is the highest form of love (agape). It's an active love that never ceases for others including your enemies. You'll notice that the text doesn't say to *like one another*, which is probably a good thing. There will be things about others we may not like, but we can certainly still love them. Just as Jesus loved the religious leaders yet disliked how they miss-used religion.

Enemies

To love your enemies is a tough thing for many people to adhere to, even those that call themselves followers of Jesus. That's the difference between God's love and our love. God loves everyone, even the people that harm and hurt us; but of course, he hates the hurtful things that are done to us by others. Jesus' command to love your enemies was revolutionary. For millennia the mantra of the time was, '*An eye for an eye and a tooth for a tooth*' (Matthew 5:38), but Jesus turned this around and told his followers, and society at large, to love your enemies and pray for those who do you wrong (Matthew 5:44). Jesus knows the human heart better than anyone and if someone, that has harmed you, has any chance of being remorseful and changing their ways, it's going to be from a response of love, not hatred and retaliation. '*If your enemy is hungry, feed him; if he is thirsty, give him something to drink. In doing so you will heap burning coals on his head*' (Romans 12:20). The meaning of this text is that a response of love, instead of hatred and revenge, might bring shame on a person for the wrong they have done. It's this type of response that can change hearts. Jesus truly practised what he preached when he knew that Judas was going to betray him. He still washed his feet at the Last Supper (John 13:2–5); and in his most excruciating moment of his life, Jesus prayed for the very people that caused his crucifixion (Luke 23:34).

In the Gospel of Luke, chapter six, under the title, *Love for Enemies*, there is one passage that is well known around the world. Affectionately known as the *Golden Rule*. It reads, '*Do to others as you would have them do to you'* (v. 31). Many think this is stated in most other religions too but that's not exactly true. This quote takes a slightly different twist when quoted from other holy texts outside the Bible. It takes the form of. '*Don't do to others what you don't want them to do to you*'. You might argue that it has the same meaning as what Jesus said, but I disagree. The reference from the non-biblical texts implies a passive love, one that says, '*If you keep your distance, I'll keep mine*'. It suggests if I don't hurt you, you better not hurt me but if you do hurt me, then I can retaliate. Jesus' teaching is totally different. His approach is a proactive one, *do to others*, the word, *do*, implies you are to be active in your love toward others. Even when nothing good has been done for you, still do them good. Treat others how you would want to be treated, even when they are not treating you in that way.

83

Care for Others

Jesus held no bias when he helped and healed people. Regardless of status, wealth, influence, cultural or religious affiliation, Jesus healed and helped all without judgement. Jesus fed the hungry out of compassion when he fed the multitudes in Matthew 15:32. He said, '*I have compassion for these people, they have already been with me three days and have nothing to eat. I do not want to send them away hungry, or they may collapse on the way*'. Jesus cared for the well-being of others and understands the physical needs we have. The most vulnerable people of Jesus' time were orphans and widows. The societal structure of the time was, if you didn't have an adult male to take care of you, then you were pretty much on your own. He held high regard for the most vulnerable, the people that society pushed down or forgot. Children were seen as unimportant. The disciples' ingrained societal beliefs showed when they rebuked those who brought their children to Jesus. They thought that children were not important enough to soak up some time in Jesus' already tight schedule. But Jesus said to the disciples to let the children come to him and don't stop them (Matthew 19:14). In other words, Jesus was saying, I have time for everyone, even the so-called, *unimportant* as labelled by society. Jesus had great concern for widows. Jesus' heart went out to a widow who had lost her only son (Luke 7:12–15). At his crucifixion, you would think Jesus would have had other things on his mind but he made sure someone took care of his own mother. He told the disciple standing next to her, '*Here is your mother*' (John 19:26–27), that disciple took care of her. In James 1:27, it states, '*True religion is to look after orphans and widows*'. To be clear, this isn't a specific call to only look after orphans and widows; don't get me wrong, it's a noble act to take care of such people. In Jesus' time, these people were the most vulnerable members of society, hence his great concern for orphans and widows. These texts highlight the care of the most vulnerable in society. Who are the vulnerable in today's world? More specifically in your society? Is it the homeless, the foreigner, the voiceless?

The Unlovable

Jesus identified with the poor and marginalised, he said, '*When you help them you help me*' (Matthew 25:35–36). Jesus showed his love for the unlovable by spending time with those that were social outcasts. Jesus ate at the house of Zacchaeus, a notorious tax collector, eating a meal with someone was a sign of friendship and acceptance and he did it in full view of others. As mentioned in a previous chapter, tax collectors were loathed by society. Jesus' love and acceptance had a profound impact on Zacchaeus, he had a change of heart (Luke 19:1–10). Jesus reached out his hand and touched a man with Leprosy. Anyone with Leprosy was deemed untouchable. Anyone who touched them was also considered unclean. But Jesus didn't allow the social stigma to stop him from reaching out to this man and healing him (Matthew 8:1–4). He healed the Canaanite woman's daughter, anyone that wasn't part of the same culture was considered a dog (Matthew 15:21–28). He spoke a term of endearment to a woman who had no physical or social contact for twelve years, he calls her daughter (Mark 5:24–34). He spoke up to save the life of a woman caught in the act of adultery, deemed unworthy (John 8:3–11). In Mark 2:13–14, he calls a Levite who was a tax collector to be one of his disciples. A Levite is someone from the religious order and tribe of Levi, they were meant to follow the path of religious life. The fact that he was a tax collector meant he walked away from that lineage to pursue a self-serving role of tax collecting. Doubly seen as an outcast for walking away from societal expectations and working against his own people. Jesus openly associated with those who were shunned by society. These outcasts were mocked and teased, and made fun of but that didn't deter Jesus. He wasn't afraid of his reputation or being seen guilty or unclean by association. Jesus put it beautifully when he overheard the teachers of the law ask his disciples, '*Why does he eat with sinners and tax collectors?*' Jesus replied, '*It's not the healthy who need a doctor, but the sick. I have come not to call the righteous, but sinners*' (Mark 2:16–17). Jesus' love truly has no bounds and even pursues those who don't yet know him.

The disciples continued Jesus' mission of love as shown throughout the New Testament texts. In their preaching and teaching after Jesus' resurrection and ascension, Paul gives us a breakdown of how followers of Jesus should love. Here are some excerpts.

Love must be sincere...be devoted to one another in love...share with those in need and be hospitable...bless those who persecute you and live in harmony with one another...be willing to associate with people of low positions and do not be conceited...do not repay anyone evil for evil...live at peace with everyone. Romans 12:9–18.

Paul goes on to say, as Jesus said to, '*Love your neighbour as yourself*' (Romans 13:9). This is based on Jesus' teaching when asked which is the greatest commandment (Matthew 22:39). In the book of Galatians, again Paul writes, '*Serve one another humbly in love*' (5:13) and to, '*be completely humble and gentle, be patient, bearing with each other in love*' (Ephesians 4:2). Paul reiterates to put on love like it's our everyday clothing.

Therefore, as God's chosen people, holy and dearly loved, clothe yourselves with compassion, kindness, humility, gentleness and patience. Bear with each other and forgive one another if any of you has a grievance against someone. Forgive as the Lord forgave you. And over all these virtues put on love, which binds them all together in perfect unity. Colossians 3:12–14.

Paul gives husbands an instruction, '*To love your wives and do not be harsh with them*' (Colossians 3:19). Peter said in 1 Peter 3:8, '*To be sympathetic, love one another, be compassionate and humble*'. John said, '*Whoever does not love does not know God, because God is love*' (1 John 4:8). This is clear for someone who claims to be a follower of Jesus. If they truly are who they say they are then 'not to love' is not an option, their lives must radiate love.

In one of the great love paragraphs in the Bible, Paul writes in 1 Corinthians 13:4–7.

Love is patient, love is kind. It does not envy, it does not boast, it is not proud. It does not dishonour others, it is not self-seeking, it is not easily angered, it keeps no record of wrongs. Love does not delight in evil but rejoices with the truth. It always protects, always trusts, always hopes, always perseveres.

Jesus extended love to all. As a by-product, his gentleness, kindness, compassion and willingness to associate with everyone made him a magnet for people. People respond better to love and Jesus' life shows just that, the people gravitated toward him. That's what made him stand out from the other teachers and the religious leaders, he exuded love.

The one thing that stood out with Jesus was his unparalleled love toward others, and his followers throughout every generation should also be known for such an unconditional and profound love. The texts I have noted here are just some of the New Testament texts on the topic of love. It's evident to see that the disciples understood the message of how Jesus wanted them to continue in their earthly ministry and what the legacy should be for the generations to come. The way Jesus spoke; what he did and his great teachings which were put into practice by his disciples after his resurrection, can all be summed up in one word, love. If every single one of Jesus' followers today truly lived out Jesus' message of love, which opens the way to mercy, compassion and gentleness, the world would be a better place. If you are an unbeliever, I say to you, don't look at Christians to get a picture of what Jesus is all about, no matter how great you think they are. Like everyone else, they are fallible human beings. Rather go to the source documents, namely the Gospels and New Testament books, to see what Jesus was all about. How did he live? How did he treat people? What did he teach and what legacy did he leave for his followers? You will see that Jesus is the perfect expression of love. There's no better example of how to love than how Jesus lived it. The definition of the love Jesus showed was more than just a feeling; it was a sincere desire for the betterment of another, no matter who they were.

Genuine and pure love demands free will. Without free will, it's not real love. If the crucifixion account of Jesus is true, it's undeniable that Jesus showed the greatest act of love anyone can ever live out by his sacrifice on the cross. He didn't have to, he freely chose to. His love wasn't self-centred but was other-focused. Many of the people that Jesus died for were the ones that rejected him, abused him, spat in his face and mocked him. Yet he still freely chose to sacrifice his life for them. To me, this is the height of love, and Jesus' love embraces the world. His love isn't just for those the world or the church deems worthy. His love extends to those the world deems unworthy, undeserving, the rejected and the outcasts. His love includes absolutely everybody and you'd be hard-pressed to find a love greater than that.

Religion

One of the main reasons many non-believers are turned off from the Christian faith and Jesus is because of religious hypocrites. I don't blame them. It turns off many within the church and it frustrated Jesus too. In fact, he went after Religious hypocrisy with such scorn as I'll highlight in this chapter. For someone, who is not familiar with the scriptures or the teachings of Jesus, their only example of Christianity and Jesus, is Christians. The problem with that is, that everyday Christians are flawed human beings. Even the seemingly good and highly respected Christians will make mistakes from time to time. Although followers of Jesus should be good examples of the way Jesus taught and lived, some of the time they are not. To properly grasp what Jesus and true Christianity is all about, it's best to understand for yourself how Jesus lived and what he truly taught. It wouldn't be fair or appropriate to make assumptions about Christianity and Jesus, based on the lives of Christians. In saying that, I don't want to paint all Christians with the same brush. I'm not saying you should be wary of Christians or shouldn't seek advice from them. There are some incredible Christians out there that mirror Jesus' love and life wonderfully, and you will know who they are when you understand and read the life and teachings of Jesus.

Hypocrisy

Firstly, let's define a hypocrite. The Greek word for hypocrite means, '*an actor, someone who plays a part*'. In the religious sense, it is someone who outwardly says the right things and shows the right actions, but they don't truly practice what they preach from the heart. They are motivated by selfishness more than love. They want to project the image that they are spiritual when in fact they are not. Christians will lapse and make mistakes from time to time. True followers of Jesus will acknowledge their wrongdoing, be sincerely repentant and seek to live better; that's not hypocrisy, that's being human. On the other hand, a religious hypocrite is a pretender and is consistent in living an outward appearance of a faithful life, when in reality they are not. Humanity's nature is flawed. There will always be hypocrites within the church. There was even a hypocrite amongst Jesus' disciples—Judas.

Jesus experienced hypocrisy at its finest. Most of the religious leaders of his day were masters at it. How did he respond to such people? The scriptures show that he didn't respond kindly and was quite blunt. Jesus' interactions with others were loving, gentle and kind. When it came to religious hypocrisy, Jesus didn't hold back because he knew the damage it could do to people within and outside the church. His harshest opponents were the chief priests and religious teachers and he sure gave them a piece of his mind. In fact, there's a whole chapter in the book of Matthew dedicated to religious hypocrisy and religious hypocrites (Matthew 23:1–

39). Jesus said, '*Do not do what they do, for they do not practice what they preach*' (v. 3). He goes on to say (vv. 4–7) that they heap burdens on others when instead they should be helping them spiritually; that what they do is for, *showing off,* and lacks spiritual depth. Jesus refers to them as *blind guides* (v. 16), *snakes and brood of vipers* (v. 33). Throughout his discourse he said several times, '*Woe to you, teachers of the law and Pharisees, you hypocrites!*' Jesus didn't sugar-coat his words when it came to religious hypocrisy. It's his most scathing verbal attack recorded in the scriptures. And Jesus is as incensed about religious hypocrisy then, as he is today with many in the church exploiting others through false teaching and committing such harmful and evil acts toward others.

Jesus was abundantly clear on this topic even warning his disciples about the hypocrisy of the religious teachers (Luke 12:1). The religious hypocrites were more interested in setting up their own establishment with themselves at the helm, under the guise of true religion. They missed the heart of the Word of God. Instead, they made themselves, *like God's*, by initiating rules and creating traditions for others to follow, when not necessarily following those rules themselves. Jesus said, referring to the religious elite, '*These people honour me with their lips, but their hearts are far from me. They worship me in vain; their teachings are merely human rules*' (Matthew 15:7–9). The religious leaders created and added over 600 man-made rules for the people to follow. Trivial things like how to wash your hands and when to pray and so on. Jesus pointed this out when he said, '*You have let go of the commands of God and are holding on to the traditions of men*' (Mark 7:8). Jesus confronted them in their hypocrisy when he said, '*Woe to you, teachers of the law and Pharisees, you*

92

hypocrites! You give a tenth of your spices...but you have neglected the more important matters of the law—justice, mercy and faithfulness. You should have practised the latter, without neglecting the former' (Matthew 23:23).

In one instance on the Sabbath, which was an enforced day of rest by the religious leaders, Jesus healed a man (Mark 3:1–6). Prior to the healing, Jesus asked them, *'Which is lawful on the Sabbath: to do good or to do evil, to save life or to kill?'* But they remained silent. Jesus was angry and deeply distressed at their stubborn hearts (vv. 4–5). They didn't understand the true heart of his message that it's not about keeping rules and laws, but about loving God and serving others. He healed that man on the Sabbath and the religious leaders plotted to kill him (v. 6). That goes to show how void of love their hearts were and the height of their religious hypocrisy; that they would break God's command not to kill.

The religion the religious leaders practised didn't reach the heart. It was just an outside showiness of good deeds and rituals and this is what Jesus attacked. The religious leaders were all about looking good on the outside both in appearance and deed but Jesus knew what they were like. That's why he called them white-washed tombs, *'Woe to you, teachers of the law and Pharisees, you hypocrites! You are like whitewashed tombs, which look beautiful on the outside but on the inside are full of the bones of the dead and everything unclean. In the same way, on the outside, you appear to people as righteous but on the inside, you are full of hypocrisy and wickedness'* (Matthew 23:27–28). The religious leaders of Jesus' day were all about keeping the law above all else. Even if it meant keeping that law above saving someone's life.

Jesus showed that love and compassion for others are the law above all other man-made laws.

Judging

As mentioned in a previous chapter about the woman caught in the act of adultery (John 8:3–11). Jesus speaks up against the religious hypocrites about to stone the woman to death by saying, '*Let any one of you who is without sin be the first to throw a stone at her*' (v. 7). The religious leaders thought they were so pious by condemning this woman but Jesus humbled them with a confronting response. It still rings true today. Who are any of us, including religious leaders, to judge others? Jesus rarely judged, he hung out with sinners and outcasts as deemed by the religious leaders. Jesus didn't hold back mingling or teaching people because of their moral status, he accepted all. The woman at the well and Mary Magdalene, are two women of ill repute according to the societal labels. Yet Jesus included them within his circle even entrusting them with incredible teachings of truth.

It should be noted that Jesus didn't excuse wrongdoing and was upfront in dealing with it in people's lives. He saved the woman caught in the act of adultery from the religious hypocrites. After saying that he doesn't condemn her, he continues to say, '*Go now and leave your life of sin*' (John 8:11). He was full of compassion for her and defended her in public. Then he graciously instructed her privately.

The disciples followed Jesus' example of mercy and forgiveness throughout their ministries by not judging. They healed and welcomed all to the faith without judgment or discrimination. Stephen, a follower of Jesus and first martyr of the church, just before he was stoned to death cried out, *'Lord, do not hold this sin against them* (Acts 7:60). He could have cried out, 'Lord, may you seek my revenge', but he didn't. Instead, he mirrored the same kind of love and mercy Jesus showed on the cross, *'Father, forgive them, for they do not know what they are doing'* (Luke 23:34).

Paul said in Romans that we have no excuse to pass judgment on others and if we do, we do so on ourselves (Romans 2:1), and James warns us about judging by appearance (James 2:1–4). Jesus did judge though. He righteously judged those who judged others, specifically the religious hypocritical leaders. They judged anyone who wasn't like them, didn't believe like them, and didn't follow the rules they made. They were so harsh with others that it irritated Jesus and he made sure they knew it.

The Apostle Paul said something I think is as relevant today as it was over 2000 years ago. I think it's something that churches, that harshly judge, should include as a directive. Paul said, *'What business is it of mine to judge those outside the church? Are you not to judge those inside?'* (1 Corinthians 5:12). If followers of Jesus are to judge anyone, it should be limited to those within the church. To those who call themselves Christians that aren't truly living out what Jesus taught.

Moral Superiority

True Christian leaders are to be a beacon of servanthood, just like Jesus portrayed servitude in many instances throughout his time on earth. In Philippians (2:5–7), Paul writes that anyone who calls themselves a follower of Jesus should imitate Jesus. Jesus claimed to be God in human form yet he didn't consider equality with God. If anyone deserved to splash around their moral superiority, it would have been Jesus. He's the perfect and sinless human being with the power and might of God at his disposal. Rather, he humbled himself like a servant. If Jesus didn't seek superiority, how can any one of his follower's just mere mortals and imperfect beings, even dare to act with any type of superiority? That's irrespective if you are a regular churchgoer or the Pope!

Jesus told a parable about two people that went to the temple to pray (Luke 18:9–14). One was a tax collector, a known sinner. The other was a Pharisee, a religious leader. Jesus goes on to say, the Pharisee talks about himself in a very flattering way while focusing on the misdeeds of others. The Pharisee said, '*Thank you that I'm not like robbers, evildoers, adulterers or even this tax collector. I fast and give a tenth of all I get*' (vv. 11–12). The tax collectors' prayer was the complete opposite. He didn't look up, a sign of humility. He beat his chest, an expression of sorrow. He said, '*God have mercy on me, a sinner*' (v. 13). Jesus said that the tax collector went home right with God and not the Pharisee because the tax collector humbled himself. He looked at his own faults whereas the Pharisee compared himself with others and was full of pride and moral superiority. It's a fine example for anyone who calls themselves a follower of Jesus not to be morally superior. It's been said, there are two types of Christians in the world, those who *think* they are righteous; and those who *know* they are sinners.

Religiosity

Before I start off this section, I want to say that Jesus wasn't against religion or religious institutions. What he was against was his followers placing religious rituals and their religion above following his teachings that are based on love. If there's one thing that the religious leaders in Jesus' day were good at, it was religious fanaticism. Jesus gives an example of their religiosity. One of the commands of God is to honour your father and mother. The religious leaders and experts of the law created a rule. What someone has dedicated to God, who might otherwise help their father and mother in need, is not obligated to do anything for their father and mother. Therefore nullifying the Word of God by holding onto a man-made tradition instead. Jesus said they have a fine way of setting aside God's commands for their own traditions; that they did many things like this (Mark 7:9–13).

The religious leaders asked Jesus why his disciples don't live according to the tradition of the elders; eating their food with unclean hands (Mark 7:5). He responded, '*Nothing outside a person can defile them by going into them. Rather, it is what comes out of a person that defiles them*' (Mark 7:15). In this instance, Jesus is again challenging the religious leaders who were more concerned about their religious rituals like hand washing (Mark 7:1–4).

Jesus said, '*Come to me, all you who are weary and burdened, and I will give you rest. Take my yoke upon you and learn from me, for I am gentle and humble in heart, and you will find rest for your souls. For my yoke is easy and my burden is light*' (Matthew 11:28–30). This scripture is in relation to religiosity. He is saying, don't let the heavy burdens of meaningless religious rituals weigh you down;

instead, come follow me. Jesus knew the religious leaders had imposed many superfluous rules and laws, demanding the people follow them. While they themselves invented ways to circumvent the load they pressed on others so as to not be in direct conflict with the laws they created themselves. Jesus said, '*You experts in the law, woe to you because you load people down with burdens they can hardly carry, and you yourselves will not lift one finger to help them*' (Luke 11:46).

In Luke 11:37–54, Jesus saw through the façade of the religious leaders, saying they were all about their 'showiness' of religious piety while neglecting the true heart of the law. He went on to say how they give to God but neglect justice and the true love of God, which is fulfilled in loving others. He condemns the use of their religious standing to gain favour, demanding admiration. Jesus even referred to them as being dead spiritually. Throughout his earthly ministry, that's the thing Jesus condemns the most, religious hypocrisy. Religious leaders should know better. They focused on the external rituals and looking pious on the outside. Missing the heart of what it meant to truly serve God, by sincere acts of mercy, love, compassion and justice.

Jesus didn't let religious tradition get in the way of helping others. The religious leaders made the Sabbath day strictly a day of no work of any kind. If you walked more than the allotted amount or carried an extra coat with you from one room to another, that was considered work. Therefore you were breaking the law as prescribed by the religious leaders. Jesus said that the Sabbath was made for man, not man for the Sabbath (Mark 2:27). He was basically saying to the religious leaders, that they were taking the religious application of the command, to have one day of rest for the Lord, too far. Jesus showed, by healing on the Sabbath on several occasions, that the real heart of the message of love for others trumps worldly religious instruction.

The Apostle Paul said it nicely when writing to those who were trying to justify themselves by the religious law; '*It is for freedom that Christ has set us free. Stand firm then and do not let yourselves be burdened again by a yoke of slavery*' (Galatians 5:1); and, '*The only thing that counts is faith expressing itself through love*' (v. 6). There's nothing wrong with doing things the same way or keeping religious traditions as long as they don't become stale rituals void of heart, or a means to an end. It's imperative that they don't override the heart of Jesus' teachings; the true Christian way of life as portrayed by Jesus. Which is to be motivated by love, compassion and mercy for others.

Abuse

Jesus warns, that religious leaders will be punished most severely if they misuse their position of authority to mistreat or take advantage of anyone, especially the vulnerable (Luke 20:46–47). The Apostle James sounds a warning also to religious leaders, which includes himself, '*You know that we who teach will be judged more strictly*' (James 3:1).

The abuse scandals that have plagued the church in modern times, and throughout history, have been a blight on the Christian faith. The abuses that have come from religious leaders upon the innocent and vulnerable, the very ones they should be protecting, are abominable to say the least. The moral failure and hypocrisy of these so-called 'religious leaders' is the cause of why many have left the church and want no association with the teachings of Jesus or Jesus himself. We see when we read the gospels about Jesus' life that he didn't harm anyone, that he stood up for and protected the vulnerable. He had immense compassion for such members of society, in particular women and children. Jesus welcomed children that were being brought to him for them to be blessed. In fact, when Jesus saw that the disciples disapproved of the people bringing children to him, he was indignant at his disciples and told them to let the children come to him and do not hinder them (Mark 10:13–15). Children, along with women, were deemed unimportant and the least of society. They were considered a bother and a waste of time for a teacher to spend their valuable minutes on. But not Jesus, he accepted the innocent faith of children even using their child-like faith as an example of how believers are to receive the kingdom of God. Jesus affiliates himself closely with children. Using them as an example in saying that anyone that welcomes a child in my name welcomes me, and not only me but God the father also (Mark 9:36–37).

Jesus wanted to make sure his listeners understood his deep concern and protection of children. In Matthew 18:1–7, Jesus has some stern words for anyone who abuses a child, causing them to stumble; to fall away from the faith. His warning is severe. He said it would be better for that person to tie a large stone around their neck and to be thrown into the sea. Jesus isn't necessarily advocating people to take their own lives, this kind of speech is known as hyperbole. It is, however, the only instance in the Gospels where Jesus states something as severe as taking one's own life. So in other words, whatever you do in life, don't harm the innocent, especially children. Take extreme measures to avoid harming children and the vulnerable in any way. This shows Jesus' great concern, love and protection for children. The nurture and protection of children is of serious concern to God. The abuse and exploitation of children is absolutely evil. To commit such an offence is one of the worst things anyone can do, if not *the* worst.

It's quite evident that Jesus held children and the vulnerable in such high regard. His teachings show their importance; his concern for their protection and well-being. So how can these so-called religious leaders get it so wrong? Committing such heinous evil that contradicts everything Jesus said and did? It's something that is difficult for me to answer. I can't grasp how anyone that calls themselves a follower of Jesus, is able to commit such evil acts. I can only assume that they didn't really have a legitimate belief or faith in Jesus to begin with. Perhaps their motives to become a leader in the Church were tainted, having a selfish ambition to perhaps serve themselves rather than serving others. In some instances, the sickening part about what they have done, apart from the act itself, is their lack of remorse and repentance for their evil deeds. They simply have no connection with Jesus and their hearts are truly far from him. They worship God with their words only and not from their hearts (Mark 7:6). It's clear to see that these hypocritical religious leaders, who take advantage and abuse the vulnerable, are not mirroring Jesus or his teachings in any way. Jesus did not abuse anyone, ever! I have no doubt he is greatly grieved by the sins committed against the innocent and vulnerable, especially from those in religious authority.

Religion, Jesus' Way

Jesus wasn't about starting a new religion. Rather, a way of life led by love, compassion and mercy. Unfortunately, as it was 2000 years ago, today there are some Christian denominations that still hold to their religious traditions more so than living out what Jesus taught. I want to stress that Jesus isn't against religious institutions, religious rituals or religion. What he is concerned about is the heart motive, when believing in these things or practising these things become the objects of faith. Jesus never taught that performing religious rituals or being part of a religion is wrong. He himself went to religious festivals and partook in religious feasts. Rather, he challenged the religious traditions created by the religious leaders who insisted they must be kept to be made right with God. He challenged their belief that there was only one place to worship, at the temple. Jesus said, *'God desires believers that worship in spirit and in truth'* (John 4:23–24), where you worship is irrelevant.

When you get to know Jesus' life, you'll see he really wasn't that religious. Don't get me wrong, he respected the religious laws and traditions but he never placed them above the true value of intrinsic laws like love, compassion, mercy and Justice. Jesus came to replace religious rituals meant to appease God with a new way of living out faith at a time that was burdened by religiosity. He initiated the true way of spirituality, through himself. Religiosity can be a dangerous thing. When you think about it, it was religious extremism that crucified Jesus. The religious leaders were so concerned about their own self-interest, they made sure that they exterminated anyone that threatened their power and authority; even if it was contrary to the belief they say they profess. They led the

102

charge for Jesus's death through deception and lies. So blinded by their own religiosity, they couldn't see the truth in Jesus and his teachings. They couldn't stand to see the multitudes admire Jesus and his teachings of love that superseded their own man-made laws and rules. Especially when Jesus contradicted those rules. The religious leaders created and added over 600 laws and rules to their religious system. Jesus narrowed it down to two. When asked by a religious leader, which is the greatest commandment in the Law. Jesus' response was based on love and relationship with God and others, he went on to say that all religious laws—hang on these two commandments, to love God and to love others (Matthew 22:35–40). It's interesting to note that Jesus responds with two answers when he was essentially asked for one. If anyone calls themselves a follower of Jesus, they must also love others, not only God. The two cannot be separated.

The Impact

In this book, I've shed some light about the person of Jesus, his teachings and the legacy he left for his followers. If you had doubts about what Jesus actually said and did; or were confused by those who claim to be followers of Jesus and how their actions equate with Jesus' way of life, I hope this book has cleared up some areas of doubt for you. This book is a basic run-through of Jesus' life and teachings, not an in-depth reflection of the true gravity of his rich life. To get a good grasp on what Jesus is all about, there are many in-depth books out there. There are also the biblical documents. The eye-witness accounts of Jesus' life and teachings, the Gospels of Matthew, Mark, Luke and John. I encourage you to do your own research if you want to delve deeper. A good place to start is by reading the Gospels and subsequent books in the New Testament.

You might argue that Jesus' impact on society, especially in the western world, hardly figures in the current culture these days. I disagree. The nations that were built on the teachings of Jesus lead the way for human rights. When you look at the nations and regions of the world that were not built on the teachings of Jesus, the evidence shows a horrendous record of human rights violations; the persecution of minorities, the oppression of women and children, racial and ethnic hostilities, corporal punishment and cruelty, on I could go.

It's undeniable, that Jesus' way of life and teachings were unparalleled. Today, his influence permeates throughout many societies, largely unnoticed. He introduced ground-breaking ethical and moral brilliance that no one could fault. Paving the way for equality and initiated the dismantling of slavery, as steered by his followers. His inclusion and treatment of women were nothing that had ever been seen or experienced by women. Truly a voice for the oppressed despite the popular cultural opinion. He drilled home the fact that all people have intrinsic worth and value, which exist separately from what the culture or society places on individuals. Jesus' way of life and his lasting influence today illustrate that true power is not from a podium, wealth, or controlling the masses. Rather, true power is from a heart of love and sacrifice—it's a force more powerful than anything to make for a greater and lasting change in the world. He rocked the religious establishment that coerced and manipulated; that was more concerned about looking good on the outside while seeking praise. Jesus taught true religion is lived from the heart; a life lived in humility and service, love and concern for others. All his teachings and way of life are based on a foundation of love, which is the common theme throughout the chapters. Jesus exemplified a love with such depth, more than we know love to be. It goes beyond a warm fuzzy feeling. It's the type of love that strives for the betterment of another. A love that places others above self (Philippians 2:3). A love that endures, even when it's hard to do. As Jesus did—he didn't feel like going to the cross, he didn't want to face the agony that awaited him (Matthew 26:39). But despite how he felt, he endured the cross for our sake, out of a deep love for humanity and a sincere desire for humanity's benefit. Genuine love is selfless, and Jesus showed that on a grand scale.

This worldwide movement based on love began with one man, Jesus. Special mention goes out to his initial followers, the disciples. They were heavily influenced by Jesus. So much so that they spread the word about his incredible life and teachings far and wide at great cost. Most of them were put to death because of their claims about Jesus' life, death and resurrection. Subsequent followers from then, up until today, continue to tell of the wonderful life of Jesus, still at great cost. Many have lost their lives in some regions of the world for just believing in Jesus.

The life of one man who lived over 2000 years ago had a profound effect on the world. He uttered some of the most powerful words the world has ever heard, that still carries great influence to this day. People were drawn to Jesus then, just as they are drawn to him and his life today. There are many who come to know Jesus and are radically changed for the better. What is it that makes him a magnet? Was it his genuine concern for people? His timeless ethical teachings? The way he lived out what he preached? Perhaps many resonate with Jesus because he suffered. We all go through trials and suffering at some point in our life, some worse than others. Perhaps it's the hope that comes with his resurrection; that there will be a life without pain and suffering, that one day, evil will come to an end (Revelation 21:4).

I don't think there can be any argument that Jesus lived an exemplary life that no one else in human history has ever come close to, or will ever come close to emulating. His perfect, moral and timeless teachings are relevant in every age. He wasn't a philosopher that stood intellectually above others. Not an emperor or prefect that commanded allegiance. Not a prime minister or president that ruled with great power. Not a conqueror or captain that took as he pleased. Jesus lived a remarkable life of unconditional and perfect love. It's simply his heart of love that has drawn billions to him throughout history.

Jesus has undoubtedly influenced the world, but it's the way he did it. In a peaceful and passive way rather than with violence and force. I guess you can say, he influenced and conquered the world, not with a sword in his hand, but with nails in them.

Other books by
Peter Tonna

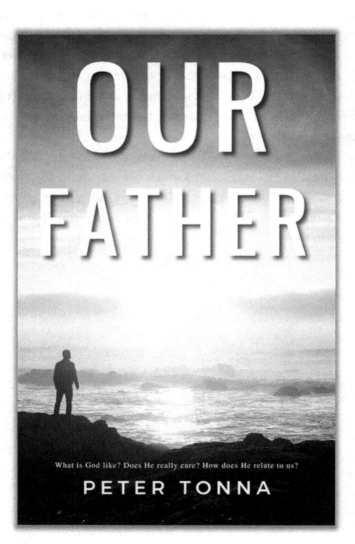

OUR FATHER

What is God like? Does He really care? How does He relate to us?

PETER TONNA

Our Father

Who is God? What is He like? Is He distant? Does He care? In this brief, yet informational book, I shed light on the character of God; how He relates to us; and touch on some of the most searching questions about God. Yes, God is mysterious but when you look into the scriptures, the Bible, you see just how much God has revealed Himself to humanity, especially through Jesus. There is more than enough scriptural evidence to show who God is, His character, and His concern and love for all of humanity. God is not a distant deity that has zero interest in his creation. Quite the opposite, He very much wants to be involved in every aspect of our lives to the smallest detail. This book is heavily backed by scripture, incorporating logical reason and existential evidence. There are an endless number of words and phrases to describe God, the one He wants us to refer to Him the most, as shown by Jesus, is father.

books2read.com/OurFather